The Nature of

Native American Poetry

THE NATURE OF

Native American Poetry

Norma C. Wilson

UNIVERSITY OF NEW MEXICO PRESS

ALBUQUERQUE

Photo Credits: *Bill Goodell* / Carter Revard
                Love Momaday / N. Scott Momaday
                Alison Freese / Simon J. Ortiz
                Beatrice Weyrich / Lance Henson
                Leidner Studio /Roberta Hill
                Courtesy of the author / Linda Hogan
                Jane Katz / Wendy Rose
                Hulleah Tsinhnahjinnie / Joy Harjo

Library of Congress Cataloging-in-Publication Data

Wilson, Norma, 1946–
     The nature of Native American poetry / Norma C. Wilson. — 1st ed.
          p. cm.
Includes bibliographical references and index.
     ISBN 0-8263-2258-1 (alk. paper) — ISBN 0-8263-2259-X (pbk. : alk. paper)
  1. American poetry—Indian authors—History and criticism. 2. American poetry—
20th century—History and criticism. 3. Indians in literature. 4. Nature in literature.
I. Title.
     PS153.152 W55 2001
     811 ′ .509897—dc21

                                                          00-010509

Design: Mina Yamashita

Contents

Acknowledgments

Many people have assisted me during my twenty-five-year study of Native American poetry. I wish to thank them all. Alan R. Velie, thank you for your patience and advice as I began thinking and writing about the poets of the Native American literary renaissance. Thank you, Frank Parman, for your friendship, for keeping me posted on the latest, and for your wealth of insight and love for poetry. Geoffrey Sill, Andy Wiget, Gita Rajan, and Ken Roemer, thank you for giving me opportunities to write about some of the poets in this book. For more than twenty years I have enjoyed the support of the students, faculty, staff, and administration of the University of South Dakota. This support has made it more possible for me to meet Native poets and to continue my writing and research. Thank you, especially, to Susan Wolfe, chair of the English Department, for your support, and to Candy Hamilton, my graduate assistant, during the final stages of this project. A huge thank you to my husband, Jerry Wilson, for proofreading the manuscript, making helpful suggestions, and providing technical assistance. Thanks most of all to the Native poets for the gift of your voices and for your assistance in the formation of this book.

Preface

Contemporary Native poetry has its roots in the land, in the oral tradition, and in history. The older stories, songs, and chants that shaped the indigenous perceptions of life are reimagined, so that when Native poets evoke traditional literature, they are continuing in the oral tradition, drawing from cultural memory the words and images that have sustained their people and sharing parts of their cultural identities. Native references to traditional oral literature and to the land are more than literary allusions—they embody life and spirit, a vision of the sacred.

This vision sometimes emerges from the most seemingly commonplace experiences, such as eating a tasteless piece of fruit. Maurice Kenny's poem "Wild Strawberry," from his collection *Between Two Rivers*, is a prime example. These "woody strawberries / grown on the backs of Mexican farmers" are "without color or sweetness" (*On Second Thought* 70). But Kenny's reflection on picking berries with his mother when he was a child lets us understand the taste and meaning of that fruit sacred to the Seneca. Sacred, not only because of their flavor and succulence, but because of the place where they grew, the hands picking them, and the experience of gathering and eating them. With his Strawberry Press, Kenny nourished a generation of Native poets, such as Lance Henson and Wendy Rose. *Greyhounding This America* tells his story.

Contemporary poetry also emerged from the social movements of the 1960s. The Beat Generation of poets, the Civil Rights Movement, the Vietnam War, the decolonization struggles of third-world peoples in Africa, Asia, the Middle East, the United States, and South America, even artistic movements such as Latin American surrealism, all influenced a diversity of Native American writers as they began asserting their cultural identities. For the first time in history, since the 1960s, a large number of American Indians have been writing in English.

John Milton's 1969 anthology *The American Indian Speaks* (a special issue of *South Dakota Review*) introduced poetry by James Welch, Simon Ortiz, and other Native authors. Two years later, the University of Arizona released the first issue of *Sun Tracks*, a magazine devoted to contemporary Native literatures. Soon there were many new Native American poetry anthologies and poetry books by individual authors, some of which were self-published. Most notable among the anthologies were *Voices of the Rainbow* (1975), edited by Kenneth Rosen, and *Carriers of the Dream Wheel* (1977), edited by Duane Niatum. Some of the new poets were first published in the *Blue Cloud Quarterly*, a periodical from the Blue Cloud Abbey in Marvin, South Dakota. Among the best first books by twentieth-century Native poets were N. Scott Momaday's *Angle of Geese* (1974), Leslie Marmon Silko's *Laguna Woman* (1974), James Welch's *Riding the Earthboy 40* (1976), Simon J. Ortiz's *Going for the Rain* (1976), and Linda Hogan's *Calling Myself Home* (1978).

Geary Hobson's anthology *The Remembered Earth* (1979) includes poetry by more than fifty writers, and for two decades it remained the most comprehensive collection of Native writing, including poetry. Niatum included thirty-six poets in *Harper's Anthology of 20th Native American Poetry* (1988). His earlier anthology, *Carriers of the Dream Wheel*, had included only sixteen.

Maurice Kenny, Joseph Bruchac, and Duane Niatum, all Native poets themselves, have given much of their time and attention to other writers of vision, most of whom are Native American. Their influence has doubtless been pervasive in the poetry of other Native writers, and their editing of individual books and of anthologies by contemporary Native poets has been invaluable.

Authors such as Momaday and Ortiz, whose poetry was included in the first anthologies, continue to publish poetry. Younger writers, such as Joy Harjo, have developed as poets, and some of their achievements have been widely recognized. Harjo's *In Mad Love and War* (1990) won the Josephine Miles Award for Excellence in Literature, the American Book Award from the Before Columbus Foundation, the Delmore Schwartz Memorial Award, and the William Carlos Williams Award. Perhaps the most popular and widely acclaimed of the younger poets, Sherman Alexie, a Spokane, has won a National Endowment for the Arts poetry fellowship and numerous other writing awards. Alexie presents a comprehensive view of life in contemporary America that is at once multicultural and indigenous. His poetry, most notably *The Summer of Black Widows* (1996), continues the tradition of older contemporary Native authors in acknowledging the spirit of place.

There are more than five hundred distinct cultures of Native people living in North America. While the poets whose works are discussed at length in this book may represent others in some ways, each is unique in voice and vision. They come from eight tribal cultures that distinctively influence their visions of the land. Yet, in more than two decades of poetry from Carter Revard (Osage), N. Scott Momaday (Kiowa), Simon J. Ortiz (Acoma), Lance Henson (Cheyenne), Roberta Hill (Oneida), Linda Hogan (Chickasaw), Joy Harjo (Creek), and Wendy Rose (Hopi/Miwok), one finds a common regard for the spiritual connection between human beings and their environment. These poets offer a deep understanding that includes hard criticism of the destroyers and polluters of our planet. Rejecting the notion of poetry as merely a form of art, these poets are concerned with the real lives of their cultures and with the survival of the earth's inhabitants.

The Nature
of
Native American
Poetry

Chapter

1

Most contemporary indigenous authors of the United States began by writing poetry. The first books of N. Scott Momaday, Leslie Marmon Silko, James Welch, Linda Hogan, and Louise Erdrich were collections of poems, and, although the reading public is better acquainted with their novels, all five of these authors are accomplished poets. The influence of indigenous, English, American, European, Asian, African and Pacific literary traditions has enhanced the inventive capacity of Native poets such as these, whose writings often take experimental forms.

Artistic expression has always been highly valued in indigenous cultures. Editor/publisher/storyteller/poet Joseph Bruchac points out in the introduction to *Returning the Gift: Poetry and Prose from the First North American Native Writers' Festival* (1994):

> When contemporary Native writing . . . is placed outside that artificial and limiting context of "European masterworks" and viewed in the larger compass of multiculturalism and world literature, it not only stands up, it stands out. Native writers are bringing as much literary technique and verbal skill, as much pure imagination to their work as any of their contemporaries. (xix)

The high development of contemporary Native poetry is impressive, especially when one considers the fact that poetry in the European mode was a new literary form for America's indigenous people. Yet, poetry allows a rhythmic and emotional expression closer than any other written genre to the songs and chants that are integral to oral tradition and ceremony. N. Scott Momaday, who has been called the dean of the contemporary Native American literary renaissance, has said that he thinks "poetry is the highest form of expression" and that he would rather be a poet than any other kind of writer (Bellinelli).

Many Native American poets deserve serious critical attention, appreciation, and acclaim: Simon J. Ortiz, Leslie Marmon Silko, James Welch, Wendy Rose, Mary TallMountain, Paula Gunn Allen, Carter Revard, Maurice Kenny, Joseph Bruchac, Adrian Louis, Jim Barnes, nila northSun, Luci Tapahonso, N. Scott Momaday, Louise Erdrich, Barney Bush, Gerald Vizenor, Joy Harjo, Ray Young Bear, Elizabeth Woody, Lance Henson, Linda Hogan, Elizabeth Cook-Lynn, Dana Naone Hall, Allison Hedge Coke, Roberta Hill, Haunani-Kay Trask, Geary Hobson, Tiffany Midge and Sherman Alexie, among others. These poets have translated rhythms that will continue to give life to American poetry well into the twenty-first century. Providing a bridge to their past and a language bridge for a new generation of poets, theirs is the living, ancient voice, the heartbeat of this land. When we listen, they help us be alive.

An understanding of the interrelatedness of humans and the rest of the natural world is pervasive both in traditional songs and chants and in contemporary Native poetry of the United States. The spirit of place that fills this poetry has grown from the inherited cultural visions that indigenous poets continue to sing. While each writes from a culturally specific vision of the world, their poems speak to the universal relationships we share as human beings. Contemporary Native poets are far from isolated from the international literary scene. Japanese, Chinese, German, Latin American, African, Spanish, Russian, Scottish, English, Irish, Welsh, and Scandinavian influences have helped to shape their visions and voices. Similarly, Native literature and culture have influenced British and American literature for five centuries; however, British and American literary historians have largely ignored this influence, even omitting Native American literature from their consideration of the tradition of visionary poetry.

Whether they considered it a new Eden or a "hideous and desolate wilderness" (Bradford, quoted in Davis 96), the early European settlers could not avoid coming to terms with the American land. For example, the natural environment Anne Bradstreet found in Massachusetts exerted an irresistible influence on America's first internationally recognized poet. Her enthusiasm for the beauty, grandeur, and longevity of nature belies her stated preference for a biblical heaven.

There are definite parallels between the poetry of the English Romantics, particularly William Blake, and Native American poetry. The English Romantics' celebration of nature, their recognition of particular birds as symbols of freedom and spirit, and their emphasis on spirituality, along with their condemnation of industry's pollution and destruction of the natural environment and rural life, are literary precedents of contemporary indigenous poetry.

American Transcendentalists Ralph Waldo Emerson, Henry David Thoreau, and Walt Whitman claimed an original, spiritual relationship to nature; and increasingly, American writers have sought the unity the Native peoples have always felt with the land. Like Native orators and storytellers, visionary poets often express not merely the individual but the communal vision. They see the most infinitesimal and most infinite life forms as parts of a whole. Whitman's contemporary, Richard Bucke, called him "the best, most perfect example the world has so far had of the cosmic" consciousness, which he defined as a consciousness of the "life and order of the universe" (Bucke 225). Searching for others who shared this vision, Bucke examined the lives and writings of a wide historical range of men and women, from Moses to his contemporaries, but he was apparently blind to the cosmic consciousness that had long been a part of the world view of

America's indigenous peoples, for he looked to none of them in his study.

Many of the words and ideas of Whitman and of traditional and contemporary Native American poets are strikingly similar. Consider, for example, these lines about the art of songwriting from an ancient Aztec poem translated from the Nahuatl by Andrew Wiget:

> I inhale the perfume;
> My soul becomes drunk.
> I so long for the place of beauty.
> The place of flowers, the place of my fulfillment,
> That with flowers my soul is made drunk. (Lauter 94)

Similarly in "Song of Myself," Whitman wrote,

> The atmosphere is not a perfume, it has no taste
> of the distillation, it is odorless,
> It is for my mouth forever, I am in love with it,
> I will go to the bank by the wood and become
> undisguised and naked,
> I am mad for it to be in contact with me. (189)

For both poets it was the natural creation, not an artificial distillation, that was intoxicating.

Despite the powerful influence of the environment on the earliest American poetry written in English, America's first writers of poetry resisted homage to nature. But in the middle of the nineteenth century, Whitman had the courage and creativity to break away from English verse forms and the inhibitions of European literary practice. In free verse and chantlike repetition similar to those in Native songs and chants, Whitman established the visionary tradition in the American idiom. Never before had a Euro-American approximated so closely the indigenous American conception of the commonplace and spiritual as one.

In an essay, "To Love the Earth: Some Thoughts on Walt Whitman," contemporary author Joseph Bruchac, of Abenaki and Polish ancestry, remarks on Whitman's ability "to name so many things with such precision—rather than just referring to amorphous nature" (276). Bruchac also mentions the influence of Whitman on contemporary Native poets Leslie Silko and Simon Ortiz, although he remarks that "Whitman's influence may be less important in the formation of their voices than their having a direct connection with that same source from which Whitman drew the best of his strength"— that source being direct experience of the natural world (276).

Bruchac also compares sections of "Song of Myself" to the Navajo Night Chant to illustrate the wonder at the creation expressed in both. He points out that "for American Indian people, poetry is not just for entertainment. It changes lives, it restores balance," and he is "certain Whitman would have sympathy for that idea" (277).

Whitman wanted his writing to go beyond the page, to influence his readers to creatively improve their individual and collective lives by living in harmony with nature. In *Democratic Vistas* he wrote, "In the prophetic literature of these States . . . Nature, true Nature, and the true idea of Nature, long absent, must, above all, become fully restored, enlarged, and must furnish the pervading atmosphere to poems and the test of all high literary and aesthetic compositions" (984).

A century later, in his book *From Sand Creek* (1981), Acoma poet Simon J. Ortiz both honored and rejected Whitman: "When I was younger—and America was young too in the 19th century—Whitman was a poet I loved, and I grew older. And Whitman was dead" (80). The poet who wrote "He most honors my style who learns under it to destroy the teacher" (83) would not take offense.

Ortiz's and Whitman's poems are similar in their expression of empathy and love for the downtrodden and in their faith in the renewing cycle of nature. Yet the responsible American must not only name but also condemn atrocities. Arising from a history of massacre, Ortiz opens *From Sand Creek* with these lines: "This America / has been a burden / of steel and mad / death, / but look now, / there are flowers / and new grass / and a spring wind / rising / from Sand Creek" (9). The book, written in a Veterans Administration hospital in Fort Lyons, Colorado, near Sand Creek, where a band of Cheyennes was massacred by the United States Cavalry in 1864, was described by poet Thomas McGrath as "a vision of damnation and resistance which is nevertheless understanding and hopeful" (cover quote).

Whitman was writing during that brutal time in Native American history that historian Helen Hunt Jackson termed "a century of dishonor." And for good reasons, Native Americans have issued some strong critiques of Whitman's poetry. Reminding modern readers that Whitman even wrote "A Death-Sonnet for Custer," Elizabeth-Cook Lynn says that this poem, composed barely a month after the Battle of the Little Big Horn in 1876, was written to celebrate the greatness of America, and that in so doing, Whitman aggrandized Custer and disparaged the Indians: "In ignorance or error or in a deliberate lie, the poet misuses the facts of this historical event in order to make Custer heroic (instead of just foolish or failed or unlucky) and, more importantly, to portray Indians as unworthy of their victory" ("Anti-Indianism" 18). In this instance, Whitman seems to have identified with the government officer, rather than with the indigenous peoples Custer had so oppressed.

"Who would have thought that dancing could make such trouble?" Ghost Dance leader Short Bull asked, speaking of the 1890 massacre at Wounded Knee, South Dakota (Curtis 45). Short Bull had been told in a vision by Wearer of the Rabbit-robe that he should give a dance to all the different tribes of Indians, and that "White people and Indians shall all dance together. But first they shall sing"(46). It is that spirit of inclusiveness that links human beings to one another and to the earth, that allows the artist to create freely without withholding meaning, that energizes humanity's most profound creative expressions. Short Bull shared a message of peace, yet, trapped in their ethnocentrism, the white authorities were fearful of any form of indigenous gathering, a fear that played into the hands of the land speculators. Ignorant of the meaning of the ghost dance and disrespectful of Native culture, whites pressured the U.S. government to implement the taking of Native land either by exterminating or imprisoning the Native people or by severely restricting their land base.

Underlying Native American poetry is a long history of violent injustices, including the violation of the Fort Laramie Treaty of 1868, which guaranteed to the Lakota, Arapaho, and Cheyenne the undisturbed use of the Black Hills and a large surrounding area. Six years later, when the Custer expedition verified that there was gold in the hills, mass violations of the treaty began. Custer's attack and defeat two years later at the Little Big Horn was one more battle in the four-hundred-year colonial war to take the land. But it was different because the Indians won. Some have called the Wounded Knee massacre the Seventh Cavalry's revenge for their leader Custer's defeat at the Little Big Horn.

The slaughter of more than 250 Miniconjou, Hunkpapa, and Oglala Sioux, the majority of whom were women and children, by approximately 470 armed cavalry has become perhaps the most often-cited example of historical injustice in contemporary Native poetry. Determined to write about things that matter, Native poets from many different cultures have lamented the massacre. For them, the continuum of pre- and postcolonial history is immediate and more important than America's literary history, which is also their context. Whatever its roots, European colonization has been so violent that widespread fear and disillusionment, particularly in the minority populace of the United States, is only natural. As Vine Deloria, Jr., asserted in *Custer Died for Your Sins*, "Violence is America's sweetheart" (251).

In his poem "Columbus Day," Cherokee poet Jimmie Durham places blame on the education system that has glorified "filthy murderers" (10) and "liars and crooks" (11) such as Columbus. Instead, Durham writes, we should remember Many Deeds, Greenrock Woman, and Laughing Otter, who were part of the resistance. We should "declare a holiday / For ourselves, and make a parade that begins / With Columbus's victims" (11). He says that children should be named for these indigenous heroes who resisted colonization.

European nations established colonies in the Americas for the purpose of extracting the natural resources of this land for profits. Both Kirkpatrick Sale and Frederick J. Turner III trace the Europeans' separation from nature to the Judeo-Christian tradition. In *The Conquest of Paradise*, his reexamination of Columbus's legacy, Sale says that the roots of the European antipathy to nature:

> are essentially biblical, found in that creation myth which is central to any society. The Hebraic Yahweh, so little a part of nature that He

actually spends most of His time using its elements to wreak vengeance on His flock, creates humans in his image and as His surrogate "to have dominion over" all the animals of the earth and to "replenish the earth, and subdue it". (80–81)

Frederick W. Turner III says, "There has been among whites a planned destruction of the past—or at any rate, all of it that did not illustrate the national mythology" (*I Have Spoken: American History through the Voices of the Indians* xii). In *Beyond Geography* (1980), Turner examines the roots of the artificial culture we live in, tracing them to the ancient Near East, "where humans began to enact the dream of mastering the natural world" (21). Turner labels the national mythology the "mythology of power" (30). Through the first quarter of the twentieth century, most Euro-Americans still accepted the notion of Manifest Destiny, which included the myth of the indigenous Americans as a vanishing race. Even antiestablishment poet D. H. Lawrence predicted their disappearance in his *Studies in Classic American Literature,* published in 1923: "within the present generation the surviving Red Indians are due to merge in the great white swamp" (36).

But the Great Depression initiated an unprecedented interest in Native American culture and literature, as readers looked for enduring philosophies and lifestyles more in harmony with the land. The Civil Rights Movement inspired America's indigenous peoples, and by the late 1960s they had begun reasserting their sovereignty rights and producing a significant body of literature. By the 1980s, literary critics and historians were recognizing the importance of indigenous literature. In *The Spirit of Place* (1989), Turner explored the "Making of an American Literary Landscape," beginning with Thoreau and progressing somewhat chronologically through the work of nine writers, ending with a chapter on Laguna writer Leslie Silko's novel *Ceremony.* Turner believes that the creators of this literary landscape "remind us to remember and to care" (xi) about the places where we live. More so than with other authors, Native poets in our literary landscape have shown us that this responsibility is crucial to our survival.

While the strongest influences on contemporary Native poets have been their ancestral landscapes and the stories and songs of their cultures, their work has also been shaped by an on-going Native American poetic tradition in the English language. Four nineteenth-century mixed-blood writers, Zitkala-Sa (Gertrude Bonnin), Alexander Posey, E. Pauline Johnson, and John Rollin Ridge, were graduates of the Indian boarding schools designed to acculturate Native people. Chickasaw poet Linda Hogan says in her essay "The 19th Century Native American Poets" that despite these poets' accomplishments, the "efforts of the federal government to escalate assimilation altered and limited the possibilities of literature being written by Native American poets" (24). E. Pauline Johnson and John Rollin Ridge seem to have considered their Native heritage inferior to European, while Alexander Posey and Zitkala-Sa described their Native cultures as equal or superior to European.

Ridge, a member of the Treaty Party of Cherokees, was educated in New England and spent the latter part of his life in California. His *Poems* (1868) praise various kinds of progress, some of which proved destructive to tribal cultures. "The Atlantic Cable," for instance, chronicles such achievements as the domestication of animals and the invention of the sailing and steam ships. Ridge viewed the establishment of the transatlantic cable linking the United States with Europe as a forerunner of "The fair, the bright millennial days to be." His poem praises America and envisions a global society, united through communications:

> For Nation unto Nation soon shall be
> Together brought in Knitted unity,
> And man be bound to man by that strong chain,
> Which, linking land to land, and main to main,
> Shall vibrate to the voice of Peace, and be
> A throbbing heartstring of Humanity! (Lauter 1896)

Poet E. Pauline Johnson looked to the past, rather than the future, for a universal human ideal. Born in Canada to a Mohawk father and an English mother, Johnson presented recitals of her poetry in Canada and London during the 1890s. Her book *The White Wampum* was published in 1895 by Bodley Head in London, England's most prestigious publisher of new English poetry. A second book of poetry, *Canadian Born*, appeared in 1903, followed by *Flint and Feather* in 1912. Hogan's observation that Johnson accepted the "European penchant for personifying nature" (24) is substantiated by these lines from "The Happy Hunting Grounds," in which she mixes Greek and Native mythologies:

> Laughing into the forest, dimples a mountain stream,
> Pure as the airs above it, soft as a summer dream,
> O! Lethean spring thour't only found
> Within this ideal hunting ground.
> (quoted in Hogan, "The 19th Century Native American Poets" 25)

Posey, who was Creek and Scotch-Irish, also alluded to the Greek classics. Hogan says, "His own sense of himself is committed to recognizing and combining the two cultures" (25). For example, in his poem "The Flower of Tulledega," Posey compares Stechupco, a legendary Creek forest dweller who plays a reed, to the Greek god Pan, who also lived in the forest and played a flute. His ideal was a blending rather than a dissolving of his Creek into his European heritage.

Of the four nineteenth-century Native poets, Hogan says that Zitkala-Sa had the most "realistic attitude toward the assimilation" (28). "The Indian's Awakening" states her situation:

> I've lost my long hair; my eagle plumes too.
> For you my own people, I've gone astray.
> A wanderer now, with no place to stay (quoted in Hogan 29).

Zitkala-Sa's solution to her cultural homelessness was to build a new pan-Indian community that would work toward the betterment of Natives of all tribes. The contemporary Native poets have far more in common with Zitkala-Sa than with the other three nineteenth-century predecessors. The only one of the four who did not publish a book of poems, she was a writer ahead of her time.

Several collections of traditional Native songs and chants were published during the first half of the twentieth century, including George

Cronyn's *The Path on the Rainbow* (1918), Mary Austin's *The American Rhythm: Studies and Re-expressions of Amerindian Songs* (1932) and A. Grove Day's *The Sky Clears* (1951). These works attempted to translate songs and chants, both sacred and secular, and to present them as poetry.

America's indigenous nations created songs to accompany every aspect of their lives—healing, hunting, planting, grinding corn, making pottery, dying, loving, making war. But scholar Margot Astrov observed that "Healing songs and songs intended to support the powers of germination and of growth, fairly outnumber all other songs of the American Indian" (19). The people indigenous to the land consider singing an essential means of assuring balance, wholeness, and the continuation of the resources they rely on to sustain their lives. Most contemporary Native American writers still create their poems with the same intentions. Yet, the disruption of their cultures and their material cosmos has impacted their songs.

In the 1980s, Oglala Lakota poet Tony Long Wolf, Jr., was serving time in prison for a crime he committed under the influence of alcohol. But he had begun to free himself through writing poetry. After he was paroled he returned to the Pine Ridge Reservation in South Dakota, where he grew up, and began working as an alcohol and drug abuse counselor. Later he moved to California, where he has continued this work. Long Wolf is one of many little-known yet highly gifted Native American poets writing today. In his poem "THE ELECTRICAL HISTORIAN THAT WILL REPLACE THE OLD FOLKS AND THEIR STORIES BY THE CAMP FIRE AND WE CAN STILL HAVE BUFFALO SOUP AND CRACKERS——AFTERWARDS!!!!," Long Wolf imagines, with not much exaggeration, the absurdity of Native people looking to the computer age as a way out of poverty on the reservation. Like many other poets of his generation, Long Wolf shows how Native Americans have survived injustices through a sense of humor. Inventing names for computers, like "Existent–1868," "Relocation Solution #1953," and "Warriors Reincarnation #1973," Long Wolf gives an overview of the history of his tribe and the continued assaults on his culture. The colonization process continues, Long Wolf implies, sometimes under benevolent guises. And as long as a people remain colonized, they barely exist:

By the way,
bring your own soup bowl.
Make it one cup. (21)

This may be the computer age, but the soup is still rationed. Hunger is a fact of life where Long Wolf grew up on the Pine Ridge Reservation in Shannon County, the poorest county in the United States. How ironic and also how outrageous that the Lakota people have been reduced to this state of poverty when 150 years ago their society thrived on the abundance of the plains and their sacred Black Hills, which have now been stripmined for gold.

Urging us to reject America's false history, Dakota poet Elizabeth Cook-Lynn writes with a firm respect for the courage, traditions, and culture of her people. Connections between money, history, and the invasion of Dakota land are made in "My Grandmother's Burial Ground" from her chapbook *Seek the House of Relatives*. Cook-Lynn refers to the buying of land as the "coins invaders played"—an especially ironic choice of words, since Indian-operated casinos dot Indian country today. That the history we have all inherited is as ephemeral and false as a gambler's profit is suggested in the poem's final lines:

that counterfeit absurdity
is no match for Buffalo bones
and dried skins of crows. (n.p.)

Seeking the house of relatives, Cook-Lynn searches amidst the artificial culture she exposes for what is lasting and real, as do other Native American poets. And yet, as Klallam poet Duane Niatum illustrates in "Warrior Artists of the Southern Plains," since contact, Native Americans have creatively used the materials of European culture to create their own unique art forms. Describing the art of White Horse, Howling Wolf, and other prisoners who began drawing on ledgers as a way to endure the incarceration at Fort Marion and St. Augustine in the nineteenth century, Niatum provides essential contexts for understanding their historical form of Native American art: "they find a secret way home / in the pads given them by

Captain Pratt / by drawing the ponies captured." (406).

The late twentieth century marked the maturation of the voices of Native poets who had begun writing by the 1960s. Hailing the new poets in 1974, Vine Deloria, Jr., called them a "bridge" linking the "glorious past with which we all agree and the desperate present which Indians know and which the white man refuses to admit" (Dodge and McCullough 12). These poets' words in English translate concepts carried for thousands of years in their ancient languages. The cultures from which Native poets live and write have long tenure on this land, and they can sing its profound meaning in visions more deeply rooted than those of the land's shorter-term residents, the "Ameropeans," as Osage poet Carter Revard calls them. Yet, like the best poets from all cultures, America's indigenous poets sing universal and cosmic truth.

The Mythic Continuum:

The Poetry of Carter Revard

Chapter

2

The mythic vision in Carter Revard's poetry renews ancient understandings of the relationships between humans and their environment. No other Native poet demonstrates so thorough a knowledge of British and American poetic traditions as he. Yet Revard's poetry is colloquial and authentic, filled with details that could be noticed only by a careful observation of the people, the animals, and the land. No other Native poet has been able to so fully articulate in English words the relationship between ancient tribal myth and modern life. The eldest of the poets considered here, Revard is a writer of incredible energy whose work is charged with a vision that is challenging to any reader, thinker, or literary critic.

Carter Revard was born March 25, 1931, in Pawhuska, Oklahoma. He grew up on the Osage Reservation in the town of Pawhuska and on farmland between Pawhuska and Bartlesville, near Buck Creek, a locale that figures prominently in his work. Revard does not remember ever seeing his father, McGuire Revard, who was Osage. During their childhood Carter, his twin sister Maxine, and an older brother, Antwine, often stayed with their Aunt Jewell and her family at the Ponca village of White Eagle. In 1933, their mother, Thelma Louise Camp, married Addison Jump, who was Osage. Their union added four younger children to the family. Many of Revard's early poems recall the experiences of his extended family in the Buck Creek area.

For eight years Revard attended a one-room school, serving as janitor with his sister Maxine during the eighth grade. He attended high school in Bartlesville, just east of the reservation. He won a radio quiz scholarship and entered the University of Tulsa in 1948, completing a B.A. in English in 1952. In September of that year his grandmother, Josephine Jump, and other Osage elders sponsored a ceremony at which Revard was given the name Nompehwathe (Makes Afraid, or Fear Inspiring, a reference to the Thunder Being of Osage creation stories). The ceremony impressed upon Revard the significance of names in human cultures. In his essay "Traditional Osage Naming Ceremonies: Entering the Circle of Being" (1983), he considers the sacred regard for children shown by ceremonial naming, which brings the child to "fuller consciousness" of the "mythic dimension" of life and place in the universe (Swann 460).

Revard studied at Oxford University on a Rhodes Scholarship, completing a B.A. in English in 1954. He then attended Yale University, where he received a Ph.D. in English in 1959. He taught at Amherst College from 1956 to 1961. In 1961 he joined the English faculty at Washington University in St. Louis, where he taught courses in medieval English and American Indian literatures until his retirement in 1997. He was also visiting professor at the University of Tulsa (1981) and the University of Oklahoma (1989). Revard and his wife, Stella, a Milton scholar, have four children. Revard has written about his childhood and family ancestry in *Family Matters, Tribal Affairs* (1998).

Revard's studies at Oxford influenced his development as a poet. He has melded forms from Old English verse with Osage and Ponca dances, and scenes from Oxford with memories of Buck Creek. At times using language forms reminiscent of the sprung rhythms and descriptive details in the poems of Gerard Manley Hopkins and Dylan Thomas, Revard recalls the birds and landscapes that have formed his poetic vision.

An early poem, "Homework at Oxford," written when Revard was at Amherst, illustrates the multifaceted state of this poet's consciousness. The student, "Crouched and shivering," has "read all night, with the curtains drawn, in this black book / Of Meister Eckhart's, filled with images of light and talk / Of emptying mind of all images, journeying deep in the soul's darkness / To the sweet fountains of life, light within light in God" (*Eagle* 75). The student notices the sharp difference between the medieval Friar Eckhart's search for God within the soul and the announcement of the birth of God by a star in an "unframed print of Breughel's *Adoration of the Magi:* so many things alive as Christ, / Pigeons, rooster, ramshackle thatch of the roof." The poem does not breathe, however, until the student gets up and stretches, puts the book back on the shelf, and walks outside to Merton Meadows to greet the sunrise—the light of the world, according to Osage philosophy. He hears "the sighs of cattle bedded in the lush grass," and, closely observing them, notices how "one heaves twice, and is standing, / Coughs up its cud" and how another's "tongue laps out / And encircles grass, pressed against lower teeth, the ponderous / Head yanks, and grass with a tiny shriek gives way" (76). The smell of "hot grass, bodies, manure, / The ghost of milk" remind the student of his life in Oklahoma—a pond, persimmon trees, red-winged black-birds, a heron, a bobwhite quail, kittens, a Jersey cow, and his grandpa—

> Grandpa carried the milk, I brought the cream, and the cats
> came running.
> Behind the garage were saucers; milk poured from under
> its foam blanket,
> We watched the kitten-bodies jostle, their modest pink tongues
> flickering,
> And the eastern sky dovegray and crimson over
> the cold March pastures. . . . (83)

These memories from childhood of his grandfather, who served as a guide, teaching the boy about the generative cycle of life, are revealed as just as important as the student's academic homework. As morning comes, the student looks at the scene before him—"here in the garden are singing blackbirds at dawn" (83). At the end of the poem, the student sitting on the garden wall prepares to resume his studies. He will "puzzle out fifty lines of *Beowulf*—that dark poem" (83). With contrasting images of darkness and light, "Homework at Oxford" illustrates the strong influence of nature and his Oklahoma upbringing on Revard's intellectual and poetic development. Close attention to the natural environment and particularly the animals that inhabit it—a characteristic of Native American writing—is apparent in this poem.

When he wrote another poem, "Coyote," at Amherst, Revard discovered his natural rhythm, meter, and subject matter:

> I was sitting in my room one night, and I could hear . . . rain hitting the roof. I really got to listening to it, and began remembering a thunderstorm back in Oklahoma when I was 16. I had found a coyote den that night of the thunderstorm, and I began to wonder how a coyote might hear this rain in his den. (quoted in Bross 2)

Later in life, when he realized that he was gradually losing his hearing, he thought about how much he liked hearing rain and realized that someday he would no longer be able to hear it (private communication, 1976). His hearing loss has probably intensified Revard's emphasis on sound. In "The Coyote," the rain sounds a melody that, to Revard, "was almost like finding your vision" (Bross 2).

Revard considers "The Coyote" his *ars poetica*—"It does tell why we sing, it does tell of how the Thunder waked me (I am of the Thunder clan)" (Revard to Norma Wilson, May 16, 1999). This account, of what creates singing in coyotes and humans, is an unrhymed sonnet. In the octave, the coyote persona remembers a "little rill of water, near the den, / That showed a trickle, all the dry summer / When I was born" (634). Sounds intensified in August when "thunder waked us" and "Drops came crashing down" on various surfaces—"dust," "stiff blackjack leaves," and "lichened rocks." There were also the sounds of "leaf-drip" and "wet rustle of soggy branches in gusts of wind." In the sestet, the coyote hears the "rill's tune" change as a rock drops and sets "new ripples gurgling in a lower key." The poem's final line, "The storm made music when it changed my world," refers to both Revard's discovery of his poetic subject and voice and the dramatic change brought by rain in a dry Oklahoma summer.

"The Coyote" was published in the *Massachusetts Review* and later appeared as the initial poem in Revard's first two books, *My Right Hand Don't Leave Me No More* (1970) and *Ponca War Dancers* (1980). Other poetry books by Revard include *Nonymosity* (1980); *Cowboys and Indians, Christmas Shopping* (1992); *An Eagle Nation* (1993), winner of the Oklahoma Book Award in 1994; and *Winning the Dust Bowl* (2000). His poems have been published in many periodicals, including *Sun Tracks, River Styx, Shantih, World Literature Today,* and *Osage Nation News,* in most major anthologies of American Indian poetry, including *Harper's Anthology of 20th Century Native American Poetry,* and in a number of college English texts, such as the *Riverside Anthology of Literature,* and *Sound and Sense.*

Several poems in *Ponca War Dancers* relate to the ancient Osage origin stories in which the people came from the stars to live on the earth. In "Wazhazhe Grandmother" and "People from the Stars" Revard ironically contrasts the Osage people's ancient and modern environments and lifestyles. Revard begins "Wazhazhe Grandmother" with a definition of the Osage word *HO-e-ga,* taken from *A Dictionary of the Osage Language,* edited by Omaha scholar Francis La Flesche. The various meanings related to the literal concept "bare spot" include "the center of the forehead of the mythical elk . . . a term for an enclosure in which all life takes on bodily form, never to depart therefrom except by death . . . the earth which the mythical elk made to be habitable by separating it from the water . . . the camp of the tribe when ceremonially pitched . . . life as proceeding from the combined influence of the cosmic forces."

In the Osage creation story, the elk befriends the Osage, providing them with a place to live by dropping into the water that covered the earth and summoning the winds from the four directions, which evaporate the water. After the soft earth was exposed, "the elk in his joy rolled over and over on the soft earth, and all his loose hairs clung to the soil. The hairs grew, and from them sprang beans, corn, potatoes, and wild turnips, and then all the grasses and trees" (Fletcher and La Flesche 63). "Wazhazhe Grandmother" is a personal version of this creation story, describing Revard's personal quest for origin and extending the literary tradition of the Osage by adding the life story of his family within its cultural and historical context.

For more than a century before they encountered the French explorer and Jesuit missionary priest Jacques Marquette in 1673, the Osage people had lived at the head of the Osage River in what is now Vernon County, Missouri. In 1808 they ceded large portions of land in this area by a treaty with the U.S. Government. A treaty of 1825 forced them to give up their home in Missouri and move to a reservation in Kansas. In 1870, after forty-five years in Kansas, they were again uprooted, this time by an act of Congress. They bought land and moved to what was then Indian Territory. The Osage were the only indigenous nation in Indian Territory who retained tribal ownership of the subsurface minerals on their land. In 1906, there were 2,229 Osage listed on the tribal roll. Each enrollee was assigned an equal share of all subsurface mineral leasing and production income. Oklahoma became a state in 1907. The Osage nation would benefit from the oil wealth to be obtained from their former reservation, which would become one of the great oil fields of the world, in Osage County, Oklahoma.

Individual Osage people were allowed to choose their homesteads from the land allotted the entire nation. The land selected by Revard's grandparents was similar in some ways to the ancient home of the Osage people. When they lived in a valley near the Osage River, the Osage had considered the hills around them sacred because they held the remains of their ancestors. "Wazhazhe Grandmother" says that Revard's grandparents chose a "timbered hollow" amidst hills, with Bird Creek meandering through it. The homestead was filled with life—prairie chickens, deer, kingfishers, and "deep pools" of water. It seems a smaller version of the land the elk had made habitable. In the poem, Revard recalls visiting the Bird Creek valley when he was a six-year-old child, the waterfall his grandmother called *ni-xe,* and the "blue flash of a kingfisher's diving"(46). He describes it as a quiet place that "seemed waiting for us" (47). His family had driven out to the homestead in their "rumbling Buick Eight"(47), itself a symbol of the transformation of the natural land.

The Osage tribe is known by the name "Wazhazhe," and it is also the name of the division of the Osage tribe that represents the waters of the earth. Water flowed through the allotted land chosen by Revard's grandparents. But ironically, the land and water by which his family came to define themselves in relation to their origins is now, the poem tells us, "at the bottom of Lake Bluestem"(47). The creation has been reversed by a society that values convenience, sports, and green lawns more highly than land that is wild and alive. The land that was separated from the water by the mythical elk is again under water. The original process of creation, which resulted in a timbered hollow with a meandering creek, deep pools that deer drank from, and a waterfall, has been reversed by a dam. Revard's family was moved off the land and into the city of Pawhuska, where it was promised that the water would be piped in for drinking, to fill municipal pools, and to water lawns. Today, people fish and ski over the old homestead, and the natural beauty and diversity of the land Revard remembers have been destroyed.

"People from the Stars" is thematically similar to "Wazhazhe Grand-mother." In the poem, Revard remembers that, according to their creation story, the "Wazhazhe come from the stars" (45). He says that the Osage lived in clans, according to their tribal structure, so that after their life on earth was finished, they might "go back to the stars" (45). Reflecting on the fact that the Osage tribe grew rich from oil found on their land in Oklahoma, the poet, looking down on Las Vegas, compares the automotive "star-strings" (45) he sees below to those above him. The plane's "wings of shining metal" fly the Osage poet to the center of neon lights and conspicuous material waste. This Osage man finds himself not living on the stars or in an Osage village but preparing to land in Las Vegas, where he will "shoot craps at the Stardust Inn / and talk of Indians and their Trickster Tales / of Manabozho up / in Wounded Knee" (45). The ironies of trickster tales inside Wounded Knee and oil from Osage land fueling the Cadillacs of gamblers are the focus here. In a later poem, "Close Encounters," published in *An Eagle Nation*, Las Vegas is the eye-ball of the trickster. The techno-marvels (neon rainbows, electricity), all based on the gambler's magical trickster shapeshifting, are linked to the Golden Calf of the post-Egyptian Desert years of the Israelites. These ironies emphasize America's long distance from nature and even from God.

"Discovery of the New World" places the majority culture in the moc-casins of Native Americans, as little green men from the stars colonize the earth. Revard satirizes the Columbus mythology of power through the voice of a creature from another planet who is giving an account of human beings to his higher-up. The non-Native reader becomes the new Indian, colonized by those little green people. Revard makes his audience feel what it is like to be considered unequal and expendable:

> The creatures that we met this morning
> marveled at our green skins
> and scarlet eyes.
> They lack antennae
> and can't be made to grasp
> your proclamation that they are
> our lawful food and prey and slaves,
>
> . . .
>
> Their history bled from one this morning
> while we were tasting his brain,
> in holographic rainbows. . . . (43)

The majority cultures become "helpless creatures" dominated by another group of creatures, superior in their technological capabilities though inferior in their humanity.

Revard's poems range across time, not only from the past to the future but into prehistory as well. "Dancing with Dinosaurs" considers the relationship between Osage ceremonial practices and the process of evolution. Small reptiles first begin to sing and to fly; eventually they "rise to / twenty thousand feet on swirling / winds of a passing cold front" (60) and fly above Bermuda, Tobago, and Venezuela before dropping "down to perch on South America's shoulder, having become / the Male and Female Singers, having / put on their feathers and survived" (61). The second part of the poem is about Revard's personal naming, in which he was told, "here is a being / of whom you may make your body / that you may live to see old age" (61). The poem evokes the mythic dimension of the dance, song, and feathers in the gourd dance, through which the relationship between human and songbird and the life of the planet continues. The human is an integral part of the continuum, singing and dancing as a result and cause of history—a "path to spring" (62).

Also focusing on dancing is the title poem "Ponca War Dancers." Set in the twentieth-century experience of America's indigenous peoples, the poem is a narrative tribute to Revard's Uncle Gus, whose Ponca name was Shongeh-Ska, or White Horse. Told from the point of view of "Mike" (Revard's nick-name, given by his Irish relatives), the poem begins with memories of Uncle Gus, a Ponca who followed tradition and customs, not just when dancing. When Uncle Gus visited his nephew Buck, although he liked his nephew's new wife, he kept the Ponca custom of not speaking directly to her, a tradi-tional sign of respect. But the young woman did not understand this and continued trying to engage Uncle Gus in conversation. After she requested that he carry groceries into the house for her, he quietly left.

Mike remembers Uncle Gus as a "heavy-bellied / quick-talking man / that kids swarmed around" (53). He was a jovial fellow who liked to drink with Mike's white uncles. Mike never understood that Uncle Gus was a champion until he saw him dance for the first time:

> potbellied but quick (my God!) footed,
>   twirling and drifting,
>   stomping with
>   hawkwing a-hover then
> leaping,
>   like a leaf in a whirlwind with
>   anklebells shrilling,
> dancing the Spirit's dance
>   in a strange land where
> he had gone and fasted
>   and found his vision
>   to lead his people
> but had nowhere to lead them except
>   into white ways. (54)

Revard's placement of lines and his use of Hopkins-like sprung rhythm emphasize the turning movement of the dancer. Between dances, Uncle Gus went with others to have a drink of "maybe Old Crow or even / Cana-dian Club" (54), but in the dance arena he was the champion. The poem is a realistic description of an occasion at the Pawhuska Osage dances when participants included some invited Ponca, Otoe and Quapaw, Kaw, Omaha, Pawnee, Comanche, and Delaware dancers.

The first two parts of the poem are preliminary to the occasion from which the poem arose, a memorial feast held for Shongeh-Ska in 1974. In the third section, Mike recalls driving to the feast with cousins who were all members of the American Indian Movement. As they were driving, the group sang forty-nine songs and shared memories. But their fun was interrupted when they saw a state patrol officer following. The AIM members stayed cool nevertheless, and they made it to the auditorium where the feast was being held. There they ate Indian fry-bread, boiled beef, and Jell-O. Then they danced and had a giveaway in honor of Uncle Gus. Although there was some between Buck and his girl, "nobody got shot or busted that night" (58). The details convey a feeling of the stressful lives of Poncas and other Native peoples in the 1970s.

The fourth section relates that Uncle Gus's name, Shongeh-Ska, is the name of his niece Serena's Indian crafts shop, which she and her husband were then running in Porterville, California. Despite the commercialization of Indian culture, even of the champion's name, Revard celebrates cultural survival in this poem, calling it a memorial song—

> for *Shongeh-Ska,*
> > greatest of Ponca dancers,
> > to dance once more:
> where Poncas are in prison
> > the songs are with them,
> > how can the bars stop singing
> > > inside their heads?
> For those who saw him dance
> > and learned from him the Way,
> > > he is dancing still. (59)

Though Revard's "Ponca War Dancers" is similar in purpose to N. Scott Momaday's poem "The Gourd Dancer," its differences are perhaps more remarkable. Unlike Momaday, who tends to idealize the past and separate it from the present reality in his poems, Revard's poetry presents Osage and Ponca traditions living within the context of a modern world that is anything but ideal. Also unlike Momaday, who keeps politics at arm's distance, Revard's poetry is often political.

"After Wounded Knee: White Bicentennial, Red Millennium," an unpublished poem written in 1976, during the same period as "Ponca War Dancers," is a prime example of his political writing. The foremost symbol of brutality against America's Native peoples, Wounded Knee, in South Dakota, is the site of the December 29, 1890, massacre. Carrying the memories of the slaughtered through the oral tradition, the Lakota and other Native Americans have long mourned the dead and called for justice. Revard begins by terming this poem a *We-ton Wa-on*, an Osage song of sympathy and encouragement. It was written for those modern warriors who took a stand against injustice at Wounded Knee in 1973, including Revard's own Ponca relatives. His cousin, Carter Camp, also mentioned in "Ponca War Dancers," was an American Indian Movement leader when the group occupied Wounded Knee in the name of Indian sovereignty.

The first part of the poem recalls a road trip eastward from California in 1968, when Revard stopped at "what some call Devil's Tower / and looked up to its top, seeing through pine limbs / sun's light dazzling in the wings / of a high ferruginous hawk that balanced between / his cloud-puffs, looking down from his blue / watchtowers of wind that passed by, leaving / the land free." Thus Revard evokes the natural impression of the place.

But in part two, Revard arrives in the Black Hills and sees Mount Rushmore, "those four / Great White Fathers staring / with stone eyes down." Revard's criticism of the four faces is biting: Not one of these "Great White Fathers" is without blame in the historical destruction of the environment and Native peoples. Indian curios were being sold at the monument, but an Oglala woman gave Revard a booklet on the Fort Laramie Treaty of 1868, which the United States government violated when they forced the Lakota and other signatories to move onto reservations and relinquish claim to the territory that included and surrounded the Black Hills.

Part three of the poem is an account of the period following the stand at Wounded Knee when people living on the Pine Ridge Reservation lived in fear of violence: "when the FBI come crashing through the doors / into Sioux homes / they don't know whom to arrest / so they kill Crazy Horse, Pedro, Anna Mae, / over and over." But the perpetrators of violence were not just government agents: "'Indian Scouts' " were "hunting down / their tribal brothers, in the name / of law and order shooting into / their sisters' homes." Revard, who had briefly visited Wounded Knee during the 1973 uprising, saw the historical violence repeating itself on the Pine Ridge Reservation again in 1976.

But the land ultimately survives the violent acts of human beings. In the final section of the poem, Revard again recalls the 1968 trip when he saw "the thunder beings riding / their dark electric horses" and a double rainbow. The poem ends with the death song of White Antelope, a Cheyenne warrior who died at Sand Creek: "'Nothing lives long except / the earth and the mountains.'"

Revard's poetry has continued to offer strong and distinct images of nature, juxtaposed with a satirical view of capitalism's tendency to commercialize everything. In "Christmas Shopping," from *Cowboys and Indians, Christmas Shopping* (1992), Revard recalls a luminous sunset turning to night sky that he and his wife Stella saw as they were leaving a shopping area in St. Louis. They had come out of a "whole huge building full of wantables" (57) without finding anything that they wanted to buy.

Another poem in this collection, "Geode," imagines the process of the formation of this stone from the perspective of the geode. A slightly revised version of the poem appears again in Revard's book *An Eagle Nation* (1993). In a note, Revard explains that a geode may begin as an oyster shell, and it takes millions of years for the stone to form. The geode's consciousness goes back to the softness before the shell was secreted, to remember the entire life cycle of the oyster and then the long process by which the beautiful stone formed: "I felt / purple quartz-crystals blossom where my pale flesh had been" (*An Eagle Nation* 92). Then the geode recalls a hand lifting the stone and using diamond saws to slice it in two. Thus imagining the entire formation process, "Geode" demonstrates the poet's capacity to create something of substance and meaning with words. The poem invests with consciousness a feature of nature that white culture considers dead matter. Revard offers what he calls "a different take on the Christian version of 'the' divine salvation-plan." In "Geode," instead of the Word becoming Flesh, the Word becomes Stone. Revard says, "I hope this suggests that in non-Christian terms not only humanity but all the creatures including the mineral kingdom are the embodied creator. The geode-slices become book-ends and surround the words" (Revard to Norma Wilson, May 16, 1999).

Several other poems in *Eagle Nation* celebrate the long process of natural creation; in writing them Revard has separated himself from the poetic tradition of Gertrude Stein and Wallace Stevens, whom he mentions early in this collection. Stein and Stevens esteemed art above the natural creation. They assumed they could invent images and people for places where they had not been. Revard tells "Gert" Stein, "You have to be there before it's there" (3). In other words, if a person looks at a place like Oakland, as she did, and says, "There is no there, there," it probably indicates that the person lacks attachment to or understanding of the place. Addressing readers who may never have been to a place like Oklahoma, Revard says, "Come down from your planes and you'll understand. Here" (3). The poem critiques the arrogance of intellectuals such as Stein and Stevens who think they are on a higher plane of thought, even though they lack the complex understanding that has long been a part of the life and philosophy of indigenous cultures such as the Osage.

In "Herbs of Healing: American Values in American Indian Literature," a critical essay in *Family Matters, Tribal Affairs* (1998), Revard juxtaposes Native with American and European poetry. Contrasting Wallace Stevens's "Anecdote of the Jar" with Simon J. Ortiz's poem "Speaking," Revard argues convincingly that the Ortiz poem is a truer representation of human presence within both American speech and this continent's "earth." Stevens's "Anecdote" is about the metaphysical power of abstraction to control our social as well as our individual perception of reality. In the poem, Stevens asserts that placing a human-made object in a landscape changes the whole human perception of participation in that place. Stevens views the jar as superior to the "slovenly wilderness." The lifeless, "gray and bare" jar takes "dominion" precisely because "It did not give of bird or bush."

Ortiz's poem "Speaking" also views a human expression as altering place, but in the form of words, rather than that of an object. As he and his son "listen to the crickets, / cicadas, million years old sound" and ants pass by, Ortiz speaks for his son; and his son "murmurs infant words." Ortiz says the leaves of trees "listen to this boy / speaking for me." The alteration of landscape in "Speaking" is an exchange—a dialogue. We speak, and the earth beings hear.

Comparing English poet John Milton's "On the Late Massacre in Piedmont" to Wendy Rose's "I Expected My Blood and My Skin to Ripen" and Robert Frost's "Never Again Would Birds' Song Be the Same" to Louise Erdrich's "Jacklight," Revard demonstrates the value of juxtaposing contemporary Native poetry with earlier American and British poems that have dealt with similar themes.

The autobiographical and scholarly essays in *Family Matters* provide insight into Native concepts that are integral to Revard's poetry. For example, in consideration of the Columbus Quincentennial celebrations of 1992, he explains that to the Osage the animals were sacred beings "who offered help in finding right ways to live in this world" (151). According to Osage creation stories, before the Wazhazhe came from the stars, they sent scouts to the earth as their messengers. The scouts were met by eagles and other animals who offered themselves as guides and who gave their bodies to the Osage. Alluding to the Osage and Hebrew creation stories, Revard asks, "Where does this earth come from, if not from the stars? Not just ordinary stars either, but from supernovas, in whose explosions are produced all the heavier elements in our human bodies; so if we are formed of the dust of the ground, that dust is also star stuff" (153).

The centrality of a respect for nature in Native consciousness is illustrated in "An Eagle Nation" as the family takes Aunt Jewell in a wheelchair to the Oklahoma City Zoo "to see just what / the children of Columbus had prepared for us" (31). They wheel Aunt Jewell to the cage of a bald eagle. A plaque states that this eagle was found with its wings shattered, so it will never fly again. The eagle is sitting with closed eyes as if asleep, despite efforts of a white couple to arouse it by hand claps, squeaks, and whistles. When the couple see the Ponca family standing near, they fall silent. Then Aunt Jewell very quietly speaks to the eagle in Ponca—words that Revard (who does not speak Ponca) mostly does not understand, except for *"kah-gay"* (brother). As

Aunt Jewell speaks, the eagle opens his eyes and turns his head, looks intently at her, and makes sounds in response. Although she is speaking softly in Ponca, Revard feels that he grasps what the two are communicating: "I knew she was saying good things for us. / I knew he'd pass them on. / She talked a little more, apologizing / for all of us, I think" (33). Moved by the experience, Aunt Jewell "put one hand up to her eyes and closed them for a while"; then her daughter Casey handed her a handkerchief and "she wiped her eyes" and said, "I guess we're 'bout ready to go now" (33).

Next the family went to the Red Earth Powwow, also in Oklahoma City, where Aunt Jewell's grandson was dancing. She and the others were outraged that they were charged admission to attend the dancing, but the twelve drums and the fourteen hundred dancers nevertheless made them feel the power of their culture: "the long-ago drum / in its swirling rainbow of feathers and / bells and moccasins lifting up here / the songs and prayers from long before cars or wagons, / and how it all has changed and the ways are strange but / the voices still / are singing, the drum-heart / still beating here, so whatever the placards on / their iron cages may have to say, we the people, as Aunt Jewell and Sun Dancers say, / are an EAGLE NATION, now" (34).

Considering the poems of *An Eagle Nation* to be giveaway items for his readers from his family and himself, Carter Revard celebrates everything that "earth brings" from his visionary Osage perspective (123). At the same time, his poems reflect his specialized literary studies. "What the Eagle Fan Says," for example, allows a ceremonial object to reveal its meaning in the form of a riddle poem written in the alliterative meter used by the Anglo-Saxon tribes. The riddle poet gives mysterious names to ordinary things in much the same way that the Osage language functions. For example, in this poem, the leaves of trees are "green light-dancers" (35). In the space spiraling between the lines of this poem, the circling eagle, the needle beading the fan, and the fan moving lightly above the dancer are part of one continuing ceremony—creation. Characteristic of Revard's poetry, "What the Eagle Fan Says" shows us the world anew.

Affirmations of Identity:

The
Poetry
of
N. Scott Momaday

Chapter

3

Author of the Pulitzer Prize-winning novel *House Made of Dawn*, N. Scott Momaday has been cited as an inspiration by more contemporary Native writers than any other author. This novel and his autobiographical book of Kiowa legend and history *The Way to Rainy Mountain* provided a model for authors such as Dakota poet and fiction writer Elizabeth Cook-Lynn. Momaday established the philosophical basis for contemporary Native writing through his observations about the power and proper use of language and the reciprocal human relationship to place. While these, his best-known works, are prose, both contain poetry, which is Momaday's first love as a writer. Though he is, like Revard, one of the most academic Native poets, Momaday is profoundly influenced by the oral literatures of the Kiowa, Navajo, and Pueblo cultures. His appropriation of the oral tradition to personal experience is a key consideration in understanding Momaday's poetry.

Born February 27, 1934, at Lawton, Oklahoma, Momaday was given the Kiowa name Tsoai-talee (Rock-tree Boy) during the first summer of his life by Pohd-lohk, a Kiowa elder. His Kiowa father, Al Momaday, and his mother, Natachee Scott Momaday, of Cherokee, Scottish, and French descent, took him to *Tsoai* (the Kiowa name for Devil's Tower) in Wyoming when he was six months old, further bonding his identity to that place. His parents raised him on the Navajo Reservation at Shiprock, Chinle, and Tuba City, Arizona, and at Jemez Pueblo in New Mexico, where they had administrative and teaching jobs. Both influenced their son's writing—Al, with his paintings and his stories from the Kiowa oral tradition; Natachee, with her love of reading and writing literature. Momaday attended junior high and high school in Santa Fe, Albuquerque, and Bernalillo, then left the region in 1951 to complete high school at a military academy in Fort Defiance, Virginia. He returned to Albuquerque and completed a B.A. in political science at the University of New Mexico in 1958. Momaday then began teaching on the Jicarilla Apache Reservation at Dulce, New Mexico. Momaday received a Wallace Stegner Creative Writing Fellowship at Stanford University in 1959 and moved to California. There he completed a Ph.D. in 1963. He has taught at the University of California, Santa Barbara and Berkeley, Stanford University, the University of Moscow, the University of New Mexico, the University of Regensburg in Germany, and the University of Arizona, where he has been Regents Professor of English since 1981.

One of Momaday's earliest published poems, "Earth and I Gave You Turquoise," which appeared in the *New Mexico Quarterly* in 1958, was written while he was an undergraduate. The poem was subsequently included in his first book of poetry, *Angle of Geese* (1974). Written in the persona of a Navajo man grieving the loss of his wife, the poem grew out of Momaday's experience living among the Navajo at Chinle. The Navajo narrator of the poem defines his existence in terms of the landscape surrounding him— Black Mountain, Chinle, Red Rock. The series of short statements, which form five six-line stanzas, give the poem a chantlike sound. The rhythm and syllabic regularity accentuate the seriousness of this elegiac apostrophe expressing love, loss, and longing.

Most of all, the narrator remembers and appreciates his deceased wife's relationship to nature, not just to him. She had been a creative force in the world, and her husband values her wholeness and her creativity. While he never says the words "I love you," his words describe what she did that made him love her: "There your loom whispered beauty" (*Angle* 11).

The Navajo man's appreciation of life parallels his recognition of death. In the final lines of the poem he determines to "ride the swiftest horse" to join his beloved woman's spirit. He thinks of their future meeting not in words associated with death, but rather with words that suggest renewal: "I will bring corn for planting / and we will make fire / Children will come to your breast / You will heal my heart" (11). Thus, the narrator envisions a new life beginning as he joins his beloved in death, here seen as a planting of the sacred corn and a rekindling of the reproductive force of the earth. Written in colloquial English, this poem is representative of Momaday's poetry in its articulation of the cyclic unity of humans and their natural environment.

Throughout his career, Momaday has written and spoken of the necessity that all humans acquire the Native attitude of reciprocity toward nature. In an essay entitled "A First American Views His Land," he says:

> Very old in the Native American world is the conviction that the earth is vital, that there is a spiritual dimension to it . . . in which man rightly exists. . . . I think: Inasmuch as I am in the land, it is appropriate that I should affirm myself in the spirit of the land. . . . In the natural order man invests himself in the landscape and at the same time incorporates the landscape into his own most fundamental experience. This trust is sacred.
>
> This process of investment and appropriation is, I believe, pre-eminently a function of the imagination. It is accomplished by means of an act of the imagination that is especially ethical in kind. We are what we imagine ourselves to be. (18)

Momaday's book *The Way to Rainy Mountain* (1969), a blending of personal recollections with Kiowa legends and history, illustrates the power of the Kiowa storytelling tradition and the continuum between the traditional and contemporary Native relationship to place. The creation story in which the Kiowas emerge from a hollow log underlies Momaday's understanding of self. Allusions to this story appear throughout his early works, such as the poem "Headwaters," which introduces *The Way to Rainy Mountain* and is also included in his later books of poetry, *Angle of Geese* (1974), *The Gourd Dancer* (1976), and *In the Presence of the Sun* (1992). The poem's central image is "A log, hollow and weather-stained" (*The Way* n.p.) in the process of decay. But rather than decay, the poem emphasizes emerging life as "waters rise against the roots." Momaday's detailed description of the scene in "Headwaters" exemplifies the Kiowa delight in seeing the world. The poet's insertion of the colloquial question "What moves?" within the formal diction of the poem also links it to the oral tradition.

Momaday's mentor at Stanford, Yvor Winters, believed that "the mind's ear can be trained only by way of the other [actual] ear," which probably influenced Momaday's attention to the sound of his poetry. Momaday's careful elocution and his nondramatic manner of reading are as Winters prescribes in *The Function of Criticism*. But Winters's emphasis on the importance of the sound of poetry when read aloud was not entirely new to Momaday. It only reinforced what he had learned through the spoken literature of his people. In fact, when asked in a discussion at the University of Oklahoma in 1977 whether one can use the written language to continue or develop the oral tradition, he answered, "Yes, as we come to understand them [oral and written language] and their relationship, writing will come closer to the oral tradition and will be more honest."

Despite its roots in Native traditions, much of Momaday's early poetry has the formal characteristics of English verse. That is not surprising, since Momaday completed his dissertation under the direction of Winters, a postsymbolist poet. Thus, in "Headwaters," diction ("scant telling of the marsh"), alliteration ("wild and welling"), and end rhyme ("force" and "source") link the poem to English tradition. A postsymbolist characteristic of "Headwaters" is its thematic summation: "What moves on this archaic force / Was wild and welling at the source."

Sensory details or surface images coincide with philosophical concepts in postsymbolist poetry. Like symbolist poetry, postsymbolist poetry is filled with sensory details, but postsymbolist poetry is more rational. While the symbolist attempts to isolate the image, the postsymbolist seeks to charge the image with meaning (Kaye 180–81). Winters, who read the manuscript for *The Way to Rainy Mountain* and offered suggestions for preparing it for publication, must have recognized that the Native way of seeing the natural world as symbolic of spiritual truth paralleled the postsymbolist view of the image as the embodiment of a philosophical concept.

Editing *The Complete Poems of Frederick Goddard Tuckerman* for his Ph.D. dissertation also must have influenced Momaday's early poetry. Introducing Tuckerman's poems, Momaday said:

> His poems are remarkable, point-blank descriptions of nature; they are filled with small, precise, and whole things: purring bees and vervain spikes, shives and amaryllis, wind flowers and stramony [*sic*]. But Tuckerman has more to recommend him than an eye and a nomenclature. His sensibilities are refined; his sensitivity is acute. His experience is pervaded by an always apparent sense of grief. He knows well the side of man that is most vulnerable to pain, and he treats of it throughout his work with respect and compassion, often with great power and beauty. (xxvi)

Characteristics that Momaday admired in Tuckerman's poetry are apparent in his own poems in *Angle of Geese*. For example, in "The Bear" Momaday's "point-blank description" includes such details as the "windless noon's hot glare" (5). In the third and fourth stanzas, the refinement of Momaday's sensibilities and his own acute sensitivity are shown as the bear "seems forever there, / dimensionless" (5) and as "pain slants his withers / drawing up the crooked limb" (5). This is a bear that has been "scarred" and "maimed" by a trap. By the fifth and final stanza, the bear is gone, and buzzards circle above, awaiting his end. This somber poem describes the aged bear with compassion and respect.

Momaday noted that Tuckerman's "attention is trained upon the surfaces rather than the symbols of his world" (xxiv), and that it is the surfaces of the world that also concern him as an artist. Yet both surfaces and symbols pervade Momaday's poetry. In *Forms of Discovery* Winters praised "The Bear" for Momaday's "careful selection of details and the careful juxtaposition of these details, selection and juxtaposition which result in concentration of meaning" and "its rhythm, which is the rhythm of verse, but very subtle" (290).

Like William Faulkner's bear, Momaday's bear may symbolize the vanishing wilderness, maimed and supplanted by humans. Yet, while Momaday's poem may have been influenced by Faulkner's story in its content and by the postsymbolist style, the poem is also linked to the indigenous concern about the destruction of species and natural habitats. Contemporary Native poetry abounds with wild animals and is sensitive to them and their habitat, characteristic of the traditional life of indigenous peoples for whom these animals were not alien creatures but clan relatives. In his later work, Momaday has come to increasingly identify his own spirit with that of the bear.

"Angle of Geese" and "Comparatives" are other poems in the *Angle of Geese* collection that are, like "The Bear," stylistically postsymbolist. But other poems in the collection are less structured and seem, like "Earth and I Gave You Turquoise," to flow directly out of Native oral tradition and life. One of these is "Plainview: 2," a poem built upon repetition of the imperative "Remember my horse," with various active increments. While the words are plain, their progression instills meaning. The horse is remembered by the "old Indian at Saddle Mountain" sequentially as the horse lived—"running," "wheeling," "blowing," "standing," "hurting," "falling," and "dying." Then follows a chantlike refrain.

The poem is distinctly Kiowa. Saddle Mountain, in the Wichita Mountains, is familiar to the Kiowa who have lived near it since their arrival on the Oklahoma plains. The plainview of the old Indian drinking juxtaposes the present reality of alcoholism, "He drank and dreamed of drinking," with the feeling of loss that is a major reason why he drinks.

The horse facilitated the long-distance, open-plains hunting of the Kiowa and other Plains Indians. Various stories in the oral literature of the Kiowas that Momaday included in *The Way to Rainy Mountain* illustrate the high value and deep regard for horses in the culture; thus, the remembered horse in "Plainview: 2" is as much cultural as personal. Momaday has said that his own imagination began to grow as he rode the horse he was given at the age of thirteen (*The Names* 155).

Also from *Angle of Geese*, "The Delight Song of Tsoai-talee" is Momaday's "Song of Myself." All the lines in the first stanza of this chantlike poem begin with "I am." Eighteen primarily visual images, such as "the blue horse that runs in the plain," "the fish that rolls, shining, in the water," and "the shadow that follows a child," are increments that complete each line (22). Together they emphasize the fertility of the poet's imagination, his ecstatic capacity to escape his own body and merge with other images and life forms. He conceives of himself in imagery that is not static but in motion, a capacity of the imagination that Momaday inherited both from his mother's "act of imagining herself an Indian" and from his father's Kiowa ancestors, who, Momaday says, when telling the legend of Tsoai, "have kinsmen in the night sky" (*The Way* 8). The implication of this poem is that, as long as he lives, Momaday will be extending the list, as he expands his identity through "the whole dream of these things" (22).

Momaday made the *Angle of Geese* collection the first part of his second book of poetry, *The Gourd Dancer* (1976). The second part is entitled "The Gourd Dancer," and the third is "Anywhere Is a Street into the Night." The central poems of "The Gourd Dancer" clearly express the spirit of place and the Kiowa tradition. One of these poems, "Carriers of the Dream Wheel," provided Duane Niatum with the title of his poetry anthology; Momaday's poem describes the process of the oral tradition and those who keep it alive. The "Wheel of Dreams" (42) is the oral tradition, circular like the creation and capable of carrying stories long distances in time and space. This wheel, according to the poem, "is carried on their voices," the voices of "old men" whose "voices turn / and center upon being," thus expressing more than individual, personal dreams. Their voices express the dreams of humanity as they "tell the old stories" and "sing the sacred songs" (42).

"The Gourd Dancer" of the title poem is Momaday's grandfather, Mammedaty, whom he never saw but who nevertheless strongly influenced the poet's imagination. The first section of this poem, "The Omen," sets the mood from which the dream of Mammedaty emanates. The central image is the owl, which in Kiowa culture is associated with death. The owl seems to embody Mammedaty's spirit, "remote / Within its motion, intricate with age" (35). "The Omen" is written in subtle iambic pentameter, a form appropriate for its elegiac mood. The second section, "The Dream," is a prose poem imagining the time when Mammedaty built the house where his family would live. Relying partly on the oral tradition for this dream, Momaday writes, "Just there, by the arbor, he made a camp in the old way" (35). Mammedaty was a dreamer, even dreaming as he danced. "The Dance" is the third section of the poem, written in a spiral-like free verse that visually represents Mammedaty's movement. Mammedaty sees the gourds he is holding as "flashes of the sun." His "inward, mincing steps" remember his culture's dancing over time as they "conjure old processions" (36). The fourth section of the poem, "The Giveaway," is a prose poem: "Someone spoke his name, Mammedaty, in which his essence was and is" (36). In Kiowa, the name Mammedaty means Walking Above (*The Names* 169). Conscious of the honor bestowed upon him, Mammedaty walks into the circle. There a boy presents him with a black horse. Momaday imagines the horse and describes the beauty of the experience: "the horse wheeled and threw its head and cut its eyes in the wild way. And it blew hard and quivered in its hide so that light ran, rippling upon its shoulders and its flanks—and then it stood still and was calm. Its mane and tail were fixed in braids and feathers, and a bright red chief's blanket was draped in a roll over its withers. The boy placed the reins in Mammedaty's hands" (37).

A series of prose poems, "The Colors of Night," shows how images are transformed into symbols in the indigenous world view. The eight colors— white, yellow, brown, red, green, blue, purple, and black—symbolize different ways in which the imagination may be expressed. Each color contains a sacred magic. In "White," it is the "white bones" of an old man's son that stimulate the imagination as one visualizes the old man leading a "dark hunting horse which bore the bones of his son on its back" (44). Although people would likely be horrified by such a sight, especially at night, in Momaday's poem the vision is beautiful and sacred. The old man says, "my son consists in his bones," which have been polished by nature. Though his actions do not conform to social custom, the old man's madness is visionary, and Momaday describes him with sensitivity and insight.

"Yellow" symbolizes the transformation of a boy who has drowned. Central to this poem is the image of the moon, whose light enchants the boy: "His voice entered into the bright track of the moon, and he followed after it" (44). Though the boy's body was caught in a whirlpool, "His vision ran along the path of light and reached across the wide night and took hold of the moon" (44). The boy is romantic in the extreme, giving himself completely to his imagination. But after his drowning, new life appears in the form of a black dog: "All night it stood in the waves of the grass and howled the full moon down" (45). Thus, even when it may go too far, the imagination has the power both to transform and to be transformed by the natural world.

At the heart of "Brown" is the mystery of instinct. How does the terrapin know to move to high ground the night before a flood? The brown earth and the brown terrapin, containing knowledge that human beings will never fathom, provide a reason for the imagination and the stories to continue.

Sumac and pipestone are the central images of the poem "Red." "Red" pictures a man whose medicine is so powerful that he is able to make a woman out of sumac leaves, a beautiful woman—"Her eyes flashed, and her skin shone like pipestone" (45). But when the man abuses her, his medicine fails and she is "caught up in a whirlwind and blown apart" (45). Only the withered leaves of the sumac remain. The poem suggests that an artist's power fails when he shows disrespect for a woman and acts in disharmony with nature.

In "Green" a girl has a vision by moonlight of what "appeared to be a tree" (45). The poem asks whether it was only an "appearance" or " a shape made of smoke" (46) before its final statement affirming the truth of the girl's vision, whether real or imagined: "there was a tree" (46).

"Blue" also conveys a vision, this time of a child appearing in a camp at night and disappearing before morning. Differing from the other poems in the series, this poem contains no blue images, but blue is the mood of the poem and the color of the light in the camp. The vagueness of the child, who spoke a foreign language and "gave us not one word of sense to hold on to" (46), is reflected in the abstraction of the poem. An old man in the camp dispels the uneasiness the people feel after the child's disappearance by saying that it must have been a dog or a bear that they saw, rather than a child.

In "Purple," a poem about the thoughtless killing of an aged buffalo, the animal is transformed into mountains; his blood, into the sunset. The people's reaction is "grief and shame" (46). Nature seems to share their grief as they look to the west and "see the hump and spine of the huge beast which lay dying along the edge of the world" (47). Thus does the buffalo become the sunset as they see "its bright blood run into the sky" (47).

A woman with long black hair is the central image of the last poem, "Black." Like the night, she represents imagination. Stealing into the men's societies, she "fits her voice into their holiest songs" (47). Ageless, creative and mysterious, she appears as a shadow and affirms the spirit. Only through this female power, arising from intuition and feeling, can the dream wheel continue.

The metaphor of night as imagination also informs the third part of *The Gourd Dancer*, entitled "Anywhere Is a Street into the Night." Most of the poems in this part were written during Momaday's four-month stay in the Soviet Union, from January through April 1974. The first Fulbright Exchange professor to teach in Russia, Momaday gave a series of lectures on twentieth-century American literature at the University of Moscow.

In this series of poems, night symbolizes the dream beginning the creative process. Most of these poems are set within enclosures from which the natural environment is viewed. The narrator describes what is happening inside or what is happening outside the enclosure, or the relationship between the two. In "Krasnopresnenskaya Station," for example, the traveler feels alienated by his inability to communicate with people around him, both because of the language barrier and also because of the social barrier that makes the Russian people fear him. Then a girl "approaches close to me" (63). Unlike the others, she does not seem afraid. Momaday imagines that "she dreams of the lindens at Arkhangelskoe." Using the subjunctive mood in the final stanza of the poem, Momaday deemphasizes the importance of the girl actually speaking to him: "She would speak . . . ; / I would listen / for the hard resonances of the river, / the ice breaking apart in the afternoon" (63). The sound of the girl's voice and the sounds of the place blend in these lines, thus emphasizing the human relationship to place.

The repetition of "nothing appeared" in "Crows in a Winter Composition" echoes Wallace Stevens's "The Snow Man." But whereas Stevens emphasizes the tendency of the observer to become absorbed in the quiet scene filled with snow, Momaday focuses on the crows that disturb this tranquillity. The crows impose themselves, Momaday writes, "In the bright enmity of my regard / In the hard nature of crows" (53). Disturbing the quiet softness of the first stanza, the crows break the tranquil dream, bringing the poet back to the real scene and to the fact that the landscape is constantly being transformed. Recognizing in himself the desire to paint the beautiful in words and to ignore disorderly disturbances of this beauty, Momaday chooses to focus on life, not art. And in fact the title of this poem suggests that the crows are the poem's reason for being.

Like the crows, Momaday has chosen to disturb the reader and to stress the importance of the imagination in his poetry. His book *In the Presence of the Sun* (1992) is a collection of poems from his earlier books, stories about Billy the Kid, prose poems about various shields, paintings, and drawings, and "New Poems." The collection illustrates the continuity, wholeness, and fertility of Momaday's imaginative work.

Momaday retains his belief that humans can reestablish an ethical relationship with the rest of the natural world. Yet, looking back upon human history in the preface to *In the Presence of the Sun,* he says that "human beings, for all their assumed superiority over the plants and animals of the earth, have inflicted wounds upon the environment that are surely much more serious than we have realized, that may indeed be mortal" (xviii).

Momaday's "New Poems" respond to that wounding. "December 29, 1890," subtitled, "Wounded Knee Creek," focuses on the photographs of the people slaughtered there. The static yet powerfully evocative photographic images of the dead inspire Momaday's understanding of the spiritual essence of the Lakota people who were killed that day as he reflects upon the actual scene and its meaning. In this elegy, Momaday imagines the seasonal life and the ghost dance ceremony that preceded their end, "frozen and black / on a simple field of snow" (139). With their "dancing," "prancing," "songs," and consciousness now stilled, they appear "in serene attitudes / of dance, the dead in glossy / death are drawn in ancient light" (139). The seven-syllable couplets of the poem mirror the cadence of the ghost dance and contribute to Momaday's respectful tone.

Momaday's identification with the spirit of bear, acquired through stories, dreams, and images, is conveyed once again in "Scaffold Bear," the story of a good man who killed himself and underwent a bloody transformation: "The next morning a bear, stripped of its hide, / Lay on a scaffold in a range of trees, / Bleeding, breathing faintly. / Its great paws had been removed" (133). Following this symbolization of the wanton destruction of nature, Momaday says, "The bear spoke to someone there, perhaps to me. / For in this cave of sleep, / I am at home to bears" (133). Thus, open to the dream and story of the bear and its suffering, humans may transcend the limitations that separate us from the rest of nature.

In the poem "At Risk," which ends this collection, Momaday writes of his redemption from a time when his "soul was at risk" (143). In a visionary state, he "lay in a cave, / On a floor cured in blood" (143). Having traveled far back in time, he writes, "Ancient animals danced about me, / Presenting themselves formally, / In masks" (143). There among the masks of these dancing animals, Momaday found wholeness again, "Remembering my face in the mirror of masks" (143).

Momaday's poetry suggests that a spiritual and ritual understanding of our relatedness is essential to his own health and to the survival of us all. In the introduction to his mixed-genre book *In the Bear's House* (1999), Momaday says he is "less interested in defining the being of Bear than in trying to understand something about the spirit of wilderness, of which Bear is a very particular expression." Momaday calls Urset (a version of the Latin scientific name Ursidae), the original bear, a "template of the wilderness" (9).

In the Bear's House expresses the larger spirit of wilderness that exists in traditional Native philosophy. Larger than Trickster, Bear "is of comprehensive mind and manner. He is wary, yet curious; old, yet playful; crotchety, yet serene; humble, yet wise" (10). The book's three-parts—"The Bear-God Dialogues," "Poems," and "Passages"—along with Momaday's paintings, embody Momaday's spiritual understanding.

In their dialogue, Urset and Yahweh discuss poetry. Describing Momaday's style, Urset says it is "very pleasant to hear, but it seems to me, well, unnatural, a bit elevated . . . high-toned, lofty, almost exclusive. . . ." (39). Yahweh answers, "It is the highest of all languages . . . higher even than mathematics. It is on a plane with music" (39).

"Poems" begins with "The Bear" and "Scaffold Bear" from earlier collections, followed by poems written in the 1990s. "The Blind Astrologers" describes the "radiance" of bears in their movement:

> They sway and impress the earth
> with claws. They incise the ice.
> Stars of the first magnitude
> pulse the making of their dance. (58)

Connected to the stars and to human beings through the Kiowa stories, bears, though blind to the meaning of their presence, can "lead us" toward a greater awe of the wilderness of which they are so wondrously a part.

Like *The Gourd Dancer*, this book includes poems from outside the remembered Kiowa landscape. "The Khanty Bear Feast," written in T'umen, Manchuria, in 1997, was inspired by a Siberian ceremony to celebrate the spirit of Bear, which is sacred in that culture as well. Siberians build the bear a house, its *shum*. Spoken as if in Momaday's own voice and that of Bear, the poem acknowledges the "wild, / disinterested kindness" (73) inherent in nature.

"Cave Painting," written in Altamira, Spain, in 1995, considers an artist's image of Bear that has lasted seventeen thousand years: "Stillborn in pigment, you keep / the posture of becoming / and are informed by that dread / of the darkness that is art" (79). This statement addresses Momaday's own impulse and the timeless impulse of artists to create. Extending his own identity into that of Bear, N. Scott Momaday continues to celebrate and construct with words the ancient and enduring spirit of wilderness.

Language as a Way of Life:

The
Poetry
of
Simon J. Ortiz

Chapter

4

An Acoma song, translated by Frances Densmore, succinctly expresses that culture's attitude toward the earth and the corn they depend upon for sustenance: "Nicely, nicely, nicely, nicely, there away in the east, / The rain clouds are caring for the little corn plants as a mother takes care of her baby" (33). Like many other Native Americans, the Acoma identify with rain and the corn, the basic elements that sustain them. The poetry of Acoma writer Simon J. Ortiz expresses a deep awareness of the essential human relationship to the cycle of rain from a postcolonial indigenous perspective. A poem from his first book, *Going for the Rain* (1976), "For Those Sisters and Brothers in Gallup," is a promise to his "sister" that rain "shall come cleansing again" (51). Contrasted with the "opaque remorseful eyes" of a woman who asks for a drink of alcohol to quell her anger are the shining eyes looking "deeply / into me into me into me into me" that Ortiz's poem promises will come with the cleansing rain. Ortiz exerts a voice for the purpose of healing not only the indigenous peoples but all of America.

Ortiz grew up near the Acoma pueblo, which is situated atop a 357-foot stone mesa in western New Mexico. Acoma may have been built as early as 1150 A.D. In August 1540, when Captain Hernando de Alvarado and a Spanish exploration party arrived there, one member of the group called it the "greatest stronghold ever seen in the world" (Terrell 88). But the pueblo fell to the weapons of Juan de Oñate's soldiers led by Vincente de Zaldivar on January 23, 1599. The Spanish soldiers killed some eight hundred Acoma, hacking off heads, arms and legs and throwing people and body parts off the mesa. They took five hundred captives to Santo Domingo, then capital of New Mexico, where Oñate sentenced all the Acoma men over twenty-five years of age to twenty years of slavery and to the loss of one foot. He prescribed various forms of servitude for the other survivors (Terrell 215).

Nevertheless, with the help of their Navajo neighbors, most of the Acoma who had been taken prisoner managed to escape; by 1609 they had returned to the mesa and begun to restore their pueblo, much of which had been burned by the Spaniards (Terrell 240).

In the 1620s priest Juan Ramirez arrived at the pueblo alone and on foot. The Acoma welcomed him, and he built a church, taught the Acoma the Spanish language, baptized many of them and persuaded them to build a trail to the summit that horses could ascend (Terrell 264).

Spanish domination lasted until August 10, 1680 when the pueblos revolted, attacking military personnel, priests and other colonists. Spaniards who were not killed, fled south to El Paso; and the pueblos were free of Spanish rule until Don Diego de Vargas and his troops re-established Spanish control in 1692 (Rushforth et al. 97).

Since the early Spanish efforts to subdue and Christianize them, the Acoma people have, of course, been affected by European and later American influences. On the other hand, their isolated place has enabled and influenced them to retain many of their traditions and their cultural identity. Simon J. Ortiz writes out of a history, tradition and way of life that is firmly rooted in this identity: "I write about Indians mainly because I am Indian and do not feel apart from my people," Ortiz has said. "In fact . . . it would not be possible for me to write as an individual but only as part of a people" (Milton 193).

Born May 27, 1941, to Mamie Toribio Ortiz, a member of the Eagle clan and Joe L. Ortiz, a member of the Antelope clan, Ortiz grew up at Deetziyamah, which the Ameropeans re-named McCarty's, one of the two villages, along with Acomita, established by people from the ancient pueblo of Acoma. Interviewed by Laura Coltelli in 1985, Ortiz said, "Place is the source of who you are in terms of your identity" (105). Growing up at Acoma taught Ortiz to see language as "a way of life . . . a path, a trail" (Rosen 173). Other important influences on his poetry were the Acoma language and his mother and father, both of whom were good storytellers and singers. Calling language a "road from inside of himself to outside and from outside of himself to inside," Ortiz describes the process of communication as cyclic and in constant motion, a part of life in the natural world.

Since the Acoma were, to the extent possible, still subsistence farmers during his childhood, Ortiz learned to plant, hoe and irrigate the corn and other crops his family grew. The Acoma villages are located in arid terrain, scattered with sage and juniper, with patches of rough basalt known to the inhabitants as *El Malpais*, Spanish for "bad country." Ortiz has written in an autobiographical essay, "The Language We Know," that growing up at Acoma, he "came to know that the rain which provided water was a blessing, gift and symbol and that it was the land which provided for our lives. It was the stories and songs which provided the knowledge that I was woven into the intricate web that was my Acoma life" (189).

Simon's first contact with a non-Acoma world came in the 1950s when the family moved to Skull Valley, Arizona, for a year to be near his father, who was working on the railroad. Ortiz's first poem, for Mother's Day, was published in the Skull Valley School newsletter. Ortiz later attended boarding schools in Santa Fe and Albuquerque during the 1950s. After graduating from high school, he worked in the uranium mines and processing plants of the Grants-Ambrosia Lake area for a year. He then entered college with the intention of becoming a chemist, although he had already devoted himself to writing. He soon dropped out of college and enlisted in the army.

Ortiz's early writing about his native culture was influenced by the Civil Rights Movement and the worldwide decolonization struggles of the 1960s, which included the Indian rural communities insisting on their land claims and political and economic rights. In 1966 he enrolled again as a student in the University of New Mexico, and in 1969, as a result of his work as a writer and journalist, he received a Discovery Award from the National Endowment for the Arts. He spent a portion of the award money traveling across the southern and eastern United States, where he met other Indians who influenced his first book, *Going for the Rain* (1976).

Literary influences Ortiz has named include D'Arcy McNickle, Erskine Caldwell, William Burroughs, Allen Ginsberg, Gary Snyder, Theodore Roethke, Diane Wakoski, Ralph Ellison, Amiri Baraka, Ishmael Reed, Etheridge Knight, John Williams, Claude Brown, Lorraine Hansbury, Raymond Carver, N. Scott Momaday, and Leslie Silko.

Four of Ortiz's poems and a short story were first published in 1969 in John Milton's anthology *The American Indian Speaks,* a special issue of the *South Dakota Review.* Ortiz had just spent a year in the International Writing Program at the University of Iowa. While two of the poems are ceremonial in nature and could have been written a hundred years earlier, since they make no mention of the changes in the lives of the Acoma people that have resulted from European contact, the other two are modern in their cultural references. All are written in the minimalist style used by many Native poets during the 1960s. Like e. e. cummings, Ortiz and others eliminated capitalization and punctuation to emphasize pure experience and to distinguish their writing from that of the power elite. His ceremonial poem "This Preparation," an account of Ortiz's personal preparation for prayer, provides insight into his early poetic vision. Expressing his reverence for the creation, Ortiz writes of the place where he "listened to the creek / speaking to the world" (7). Cutting prayer sticks, he felt "sorrow in leaving / fresh wounds in growing things." The poem translates into language the sensory knowledge of the creek and the sticks: "i smelled its smell / which are words also" (7).

According to the Acoma cosmology, Iatiku, one of two original human beings, both of whom were female, made prayer sticks for each type of katsina or spirit and taught her children how to make the prayer sticks and how to pray to the spirits of the four seasons, using appropriate prayers and prayer sticks (Stirling 15–17). In the poem, Ortiz affirms the spiritual attitude of his people, his own reverence for the earth, and the belief that "prayers / make things possible" ("The Preparation" 7).

"Smoking My Prayers," another poem from the anthology, expresses the symbolic reciprocity of smoking—spirit and life entering with the inhaled breath, the exhaled breath returning them to the atmosphere. In the Acoma creation story, Tsichtinako (Thought-Woman) taught the people to plant tobacco, as well as how to roll the tobacco leaves in corn husks and how to smoke. The Acoma believe that their prayers enter the realm of the spirits through the smoke (Stirling 6–7). Addressing the spirits, Ortiz's poem ends, "i have become whole and strong with yourself / this morning i am living with your breath" (8).

Ortiz's other two poems in *The American Indian Speaks* consider the superficial notions of history and Native culture that are prevalent in the United States. "Irish Poets on Saturday and an Indian" comments on how odd it feels to Native people when they find themselves "making prayers in literary journals." It is a "strange world now," Ortiz says (6). The poem's final lines express the suppressed truth that liquor can sometimes translate into words: "in their minds the anger and madness / will come forth in tongues and fury" (6).

Other magazines soon published Ortiz's poetry, including *Dakotah Territory, Greenfield Review, Pembroke Magazine,* and *The Indian Historian.* His poems were also included in anthologies, such as Faderman and Bradshaw's *Speaking for Ourselves,* Niatum's *Carriers of the Dream Wheel,* Allen's *The Whispering Wind,* and Dodge and McCullough's *Voices from Wah'kon-tah.*

His poem "Relocation," which appeared in Shirley Hill Witt and Stan Steiner's *The Way: An Anthology of American Indian Literature,* is a direct statement of an American Indian's alienation in the city, away from tribal land. Within the poem is contained the history of a man "armed with a pint of wine / i cheated my children to buy" (85). The poem shows, from a Native perspective, the effects of the Eisenhower Administration's attempts to move American Indians off their reservations and into cities. In 1953, after the U.S. Congress decided that the Indian tribes should be terminated, eleven tribes were officially declared to be nonexistent. The Interior Department then adopted rules allowing non-Indians to lease tribal lands.

When most tribes resisted termination, the federal government began a program to relocate Indians into large cities and find them jobs. By the 1970s the relocation program had been so "successful" that approximately half of all American Indians lived in cities (Witt and Steiner 82). The narrator of Ortiz's "Relocation" speaks from the bitter experience of an urban Indian being mistaught that his native "corn & potatoes and chili and mutton / did not nourish" him. In the polluted city he is "lonely for hills / . . . lonely for myself" (85).

Ortiz included "Relocation" and many other previously published poems in *Going for the Rain* (1976), one of a series of Native American books published by Harper & Row. This collection and two later ones, *A Good Journey* (1977) and *Fight Back* (1980), were merged into a single volume, *Woven Stone*, in 1992. With this title Ortiz draws an analogy between building a wall in the ancient Acoma way practiced by his father and his own construction of poetry. The concept of woven stone is related in "The Story of How a Wall Stands" from *Going for the Rain* and in "This Occurs to Me" from *A Good Journey*. As he recalls the stories and knowledge passed on to him, Ortiz recognizes the beauty and usefulness of the earth and says that he learns to build his poems by watching the animals, allowing his mind to create "a vision of weaving things / inwardly and outwardly" (*Woven Stone* 265).

Considered in the larger tradition of American poetry, *Going for the Rain* stands in sharp contrast to T. S. Eliot's "The Waste Land," even though the land from which Ortiz's voice emerged is in fact far more arid than the Missouri or the London of Eliot. While the personae of Eliot's poem are individuals alienated from their culture and even the earth, Ortiz's persona, which seems to closely parallel his own consciousness, views the land and people as related and part of a larger cycle of nature.

Cyclic in structure, *Going for the Rain* has four parts: "Preparation," "Leaving," "Returning," and "The Rain Falls." A paraphrase of the book as a whole, the Prologue begins with a traditional song about going "for the shiwana," or rain-bearing spirits. The following four paragraphs explain the significance to his life and all life of four things—"A man makes his prayers," "A man leaves," "A man returns," and "The rain comes and falls." Like Leslie

Silko's novel *Ceremony*, this book was conceived as a human enactment of the sacred process of the creation.

"The Creation According to Coyote," the first poem in "Preparation," seems to be a retelling of a story Ortiz had heard from an uncle. Ortiz's colloquial, light-hearted narrative echoes traditional stories told of the clever, mischievous coyote that befriended the original human beings. The creation story of the coyote is similar to the previously mentioned creation story recorded by Stirling, but instead of two sisters, the focus here is on twin brothers, whose actions were essential in the epochs following the emergence. In both stories, human beings emerged from the earth. In Ortiz's visibly dramatic version of the emergence of the Acoma people, "your black head burst from granite" (*Going for the Rain* 3).

"Preparation" is about Ortiz's appreciation of the place he has come from and the people he is close to in that place. To the Acoma, all of life, including personal relationships, is part of the continuum of creation. Ortiz's children, Raho Nez and Rainy Dawn, are particularly important in his early poems. In "Preparation," Ortiz frequently refers to his son and daughter, to his anticipation of their births, and to his desire to prepare them for their life's journey so they will live with a feeling of respect, in good relation to the creation. He also emphasizes the influence of older relatives on children in poems such as "My Father's Song," which recalls his father unearthing a nest of mice when planting corn. Instead of killing the "tiny pink animals" (20), Ortiz's father scooped them up and put them at the edge of the field so that they could live, a gesture that taught his son to protect and value new life. The "Preparation" poems are like prayers, revealing a reverent and passionate love for the land.

The poems in the second part of the book, "Leaving," view traveling as a way to learn more of the relationships one shares with all people and places. Leaving also is a necessary part of growth. Ortiz's "traveling is a prayer as well, and he must keep on" (xiii). Leaving is a way to expand one's conscience and remain vital and alive. In "Travels in the South," Ortiz records the development of his social consciousness of America through traveling in the area of the United States most associated with extremes of hospitality on the one hand and bigotry on the other. Traveling through the South made him conscious not only of the other Native Americans living in the area but of the region's racism against African Americans. The three sections of this poem—"East Texas," "The Creek Nation East of the Mississippi," and "Crossing the Georgia Border into Florida"—represent some places where Ortiz felt a strong sense of relatedness to the land and the people living on the land, and other places where he felt the alienation and loss of Native people in the prisons and cities.

Having been welcomed by the Alabama-Coushatta people, he then traveled into Texas. In Dallas, when he asked a white federal employee the number of Indians in that city, the man looked at him suspiciously and said, "they come every week"(34). He saw a Navajo welder who was out of work and an "Apache woman crying for her lost life." At Caddo Lake, he met a park ranger who told him that the Caddo "used to be some Indian tribe" and "two Black women fishing at the lake" were "good to be with" (34). "East Texas" ends with a prayer "for strength and the Caddo and the Black women / and my young son at home and Dallas and when / it would be the morning, the sun." Thus have Ortiz's travels expanded his prayers and his vision of relationships.

The second section of this poem, "The Creek Nation East of the Mississippi," has at its core a visit with a Creek man, Chief Alvin McGee. Chief McGee showed Ortiz his seventy acres of garden and fields near Atmore, Alabama, and told Ortiz about the Creek leader Osceola. People kept coming to McGee's house to lobby for their candidates. It was 1970, and Alabama Governor George Wallace was up for reelection. Recognizing McGee's concern about the racist politics of that time and place, Ortiz said in farewell, "Keep together, please don't worry about Wallace." McGee, who embraced Ortiz and blessed him, reminded the poet of his own grandfather and of the land around Acoma. As the section ends, Ortiz recalls that as he was leaving, on the freeway to Atlanta, his car radio reported the killings at Kent State, and he stopped just past a sign reading "NO STOPPING EXCEPT IN CASE OF / EMERGENCY / and hugged a tree" (36). The poem conveys the national and personal trauma of that May 4, when four students were killed by National Guardsmen during a protest against the Vietnam War on the Kent State University campus.

Traveling awakens one to personal, social, and political reality. For a Native American, this reality often includes being a target of racism. In the third section, "Crossing the Georgia Border into Florida," Ortiz goes to Atlanta, worrying about the length of his hair, which was past his ears, like his grandfather's. When the desk clerk at the "classy" hotel where he would stay for an Indian meeting was reluctant to book him a room, the narrator "figured I'm sure glad / that I'm not a Black man" (36). Later, having entered Florida, Ortiz paid an entrance fee into a state park which the ranger said was "noted for the Indians / that don't live here anymore" (37). Trying to make friends with a squirrel and a red bird, he scattered some stale white bread crumbs on the ground for them. The lines "They didn't take the crumbs, / and I didn't blame them" (37) obliquely refer to the government's attempts to appease minorities with undesirable crumbs, rather than real opportunities to thrive.

In a number of poems in the "Leaving" and "Returning" parts of *Going for the Rain,* Ortiz contrasts life in the city to life in the natural environment. The third section, "Returning," is parallel to leaving. Both produce emotional as well as rational changes in one's vision. Ortiz's concern for the alienation, loneliness, and purposelessness he saw in the cities across the South made him consider the causes of and solutions for this despair. With Ortiz's awareness of ancient Acoma traditions and values now enhanced by his increasing social and political awareness, these poems critique technological, capitalist society. Native schoolchildren are fed "canned food, Dick & Jane textbooks, IBM cards, Western philosophies, General Electric" (72) and with them the notion that Western civilization is superior to their Acoma culture's life on the land. "The Significance of a Veteran's Day" asks how Native people can feel significant in American society when American Indian children see their ancestors presented in textbooks as historical savages, noble or otherwise, or when they do not see them at all, but only Dick and Jane. Irony pervades this poem. Defining both "significance" and "veteran" from an Acoma perspective, Ortiz explores the meaning and history behind our war veterans. The Indian veteran finds himself "waking up on concrete," homeless in a land where his people have lived "at least 30,000 years" as they "traveled with the monumental yearning / of glaciers" (72). Traveling brought Ortiz renewed respect for his people, who were "able / to survive insignificance" (72).

The fourth part of *Going for the Rain*, "The Rain Falls," completes the cyclic journey as the Acoma people wait for rain. In several poems Ortiz's children represent new beginnings as the cycle of life continues. "Four Rains" is dedicated to Ortiz's baby daughter, Rainy Dawn, who symbolizes the life-bringing rain. In "First Rain" it is the baby's "brighteyed" look and the "mountains shining / when light slants"(107) into "delicate" roots that reflect the visual and symbolic nurturing of a spring rain.

In "Second Rain" the imagery is auditory. The child begins to speak, naming the things around her, a delight to those who live on dry land, and like the sound of rain to those who love her.

"Third Rain" begins with a "Brighteyed flash" descriptive of Rainy Dawn, but this section of the poem is about the baby girl in relationship to the earth and the knowledge accumulated by her ancestors over the ages "reaching back / into granite," their origin (107). The rain, the granite, and the child are all "magic and mysteries" of nature.

Finally, in "Fourth Rain" Ortiz speaks to the shiwana. Rainy Dawn is the present symbol of the rain, but since the full meaning of rain and the prelanguage utterances of a baby cannot be spoken but can be understood only intuitively, the poem ends "I know" (108).

Going for the Rain describes a cyclic journey, not a goal, and several poems in "The Rain Falls" describe the essential continuation of that cycle. In "For Joy to Leave Upon," Ortiz remembers cutting his grandfather's grapevines "down to the quick" (111) so they could produce new life. This pruning symbolizes the necessity for a separation between human beings, to allow them a chance for new life, for "green new shoots" to develop.

Though he had initially arranged his early poems in a single manuscript, an editor at Harper & Row told him a three-hundred-page book by an unknown poet was not feasible, so Ortiz divided the manuscript into two books, *Going for the Rain* and his next book, *A Good Journey*. In his short introduction to the "Good Journey" section of *Woven Stone*, he says that in this collection he wanted to "translate" the power of the spoken word into written narrative. The poems in *A Good Journey*, more obviously linked to the oral tradition than those in his first book, are grouped into five parts: "Telling," "Notes for My Child," "How Much He Remembered," "Will Come Forth in Tongues and Fury," and "I Tell You Now." The voice of these poems is colloquial, a style the Beat poets helped Ortiz accomplish. In "Telling About Coyote," who is always on the move, Ortiz writes, "I saw him somewhere/ . . . / heading for Tulsy Town I guess / just trucking along" (*Woven Stone* 159–60). Animals inhabit many of the poems in this book—Coyote, Crow, Dog, Wolf, Magpie, Skunk, Owl, Blue Jay, Gold Finch, Squirrel, and Ant—and all must be accepted as relatives: "'One can't be too choosey,' said Crow" (161). Down to earth (natural in their language) and sometimes humorous, these poems are about everyday experience and its cosmic significance. In "How to make a good chili stew . . . ," Ortiz says, "you should pay the utmost attention to everything, and that means / the earth, clouds, sounds, the wind. All these go into the cooking" (175). In all of life, including ordinary domestic work, one should be aware of one's natural surroundings.

It is when that awareness is disturbed that one becomes fragmented and lost. "A San Diego Poem: January–February 1973" is a statement of the discomfort Ortiz felt flying from his Southwest home to California. As the plane approached the airport, he felt the prayers of his "native selfhood / . . . strangled in my throat" (165). Later, in "Under the L.A. International Airport," he felt lost, even though he knew where he was: "America has finally caught me. / I meld into the walls of that tunnel / and become the silent burial. There are no echoes" (167). These lines strangely echo Poe's gothic imagery. The airport is also a perfect symbol of the fast-paced, highly technological environment of urban life. Such physical and societal structures can isolate us from our natural surroundings and from one another, and cause us to lose touch with our physical and spiritual place.

In contrast, when Ortiz lay down on his "earth bed" in "Grand Canyon Christmas Eve 1969," he found it "possible / to believe legend . . . / to believe eternity" (188). This poem introduces the second part of the book, "Notes for My Child," which celebrates birth and the joy and hopefulness of children. Some of these are alternative versions of poems in *Going for the Rain*. Within the poem "Notes for My Child" is a shorter poem, "To Insure Survival," for his daughter Rainy Dawn, who was born in 1973. The lines

"You come forth / the color of a stone cliff / at dawn" (195) picture the emerging child as the earth, the earth as the child. The poem that follows, "Earth and Rain, The Plants & Sun," announces the cultural blessing brought by the katsina, "The plants with bells. / The stones with voices," who arrive dancing with prayers for the child. These poems are a song of hope and determination that "It shall continue well" (213) for the child and for all of us.

The third part, "How Much He Remembered," groups poems of love, loss, loneliness, and wandering. The poems chronicle the pain and alienation that are part of life, even if one is not separated from the natural world. Beginning with "Woman, This Indian Woman" and ending with "Two Coyote Ones," these poems are about relationships with a number of women, Indian and non-Indian, and ultimately with one's entire social and political environment. The voice is alternately sad, disengaged, celebratory, and cynical.

Ortiz's question, "Was it a good place to die, / someplace called Kent State USA?" in the poem "Morning By a Lakeside in Marion County, S.C.," provides a transition to the fourth part of the book. The line "Was it a good place to die," which modifies the war cry "It's a good day to die," compares the deaths of student protesters with those of Lakota warriors in the nineteenth-century wars on the plains. Though neither the students nor the warriors should have been forced to die, Ortiz honors their loss.

The fourth part, "Will Come Forth in Tongues and Fury," anticipates Ortiz's book *Fight Back*. The poems tell the political history of the taking of Indian land by the federal government and by industry and describe the destructive impact of technological development. In "Vision Shadows," the animal and spiritual habitat are injured as "Poisonous fumes cross our sacred paths" (245). And the human animal suffers also, often turning to alcohol for some kind of relief from loss and poverty, as in "Time to Kill in Gallup." Here Ortiz writes of a woman who in "Gumming back sorrow, / . . . gags on wine" (248). But out of this desperate portrait, Ortiz builds a vision of hope that begins when he calls her "Sister." "The People will rise" (250), the poem asserts, but only if they ask for real, not spare, change.

In *"'The State's claim that it seeks in no way to deprive Indians of their rightful share of water, but only to define that share, falls on deaf ears,'"* a satirical title quoted from a 1974 editorial in the *Albuquerque Journal*, Ortiz writes of the negative impact of "Railroads," "Gas Lines," "Highways," "Phone Company," "Cable TV," and "Right of Way" on himself and the Acoma people. Since encroachment on the land and culture by these and other entities seems inevitable, Ortiz sees stories of the people's birth, growing, struggles, and history and their prayers as essential—the "only way" they can survive.

And so, it is with an emphasis on telling stories that the book ends, in the fifth part, "I Tell You Now." People like Amado Quintana, whom the people call "Old Man Humped Back" in the poem "When It Was Taking Place," are the transmitters of cultural history. Quintana remembered such accomplishments as the building of an irrigation canal from the river to the fields when he was a child. The stories of "carrying / his father's hand-made shovel" and of his mother, who, when he and his father returned, "would grab them and hold them / strongly to her" (269), showed Quintana's grandson the historical human investment that produced the prosperity of his culture.

But finally, it is all the people who love the earth, not only the Acoma people, that Ortiz wants to help survive. His "Poems from the Veterans Hospital," which anticipate his book *From Sand Creek*, are about life inside and outside the hospital for a number of veterans who, like Ortiz, are there to overcome their addiction to alcohol. These men can relate to one another; and through observing each other and sharing stories, they grow to care for each other and to feel a sense of community. In "For a Taos Man Heading South," a white V.A. psychologist says "'I wish you / weren't going back into the same environment'" (280). Ortiz writes, "Mondragon and I had to tell him, 'That's our home, our land, our people. That's our life.'"

Ortiz's engaging message is of commitment and continuance, maintained through many forms of resistance. *Fight Back: For the Sake of the People, For the Sake of the Land*, published in 1980 to commemorate the Pueblo Revolt of 1680, develops this theme by placing the lives of people working for corporate America during the 1950s and 1960s within the context of America's history of colonial and capitalist domination. That life has not been easy for the Acoma and other Indians of the Southwest is a fact of history pictured powerfully in this book. The most political and experimental of his volumes,

Fight Back is a blending of poetry and prose, a style that Native poets Joy Harjo, Sherman Alexie, and others would use in later books.

The book opens with "Mid-America Prayer." Here the solidarity of human beings with "all items of life" is seen as necessary "for the continuance of life" (1). Much of the book is autobiographical prose in which Ortiz relates his own work experience to that of his father, who told Ortiz and his brothers "to never work for the railroad and do the grueling labor he had to do in order to make a living" (2). Ortiz did not work on the railroad, but he did work in the uranium mines and mills that opened in the Acoma and Laguna area in the 1950s and 1960s. Many of the *Fight Back* poems are about the mine workers, their relationships to one another, and their callous treatment by the industry and by American society.

"It Was That Indian" illustrates with bitter irony the way American society has exploited Native people. Martinez, a Navajo man who "discovered uranium / west of Grants" (2), was "celebrated" for a time, until people started complaining about the toxic chemicals, overcrowding, cave-ins, high cost of living, and radiation that resulted from uranium mining. Then they had someone to blame, not the industry that had used him for self-promotion but "that Indian who started that boom" (3).

The promise of social mobility rang false, as Acoma and Laguna men working at Ambrosia Lake and at Jackpile remained in the worst jobs, thirty years after being promised that they could work their way up. Most poignant is "Ray's Story," about an Indian man who was pulled "right down into the jaws / of that crusher" (9). When the cable Lacey was trying to pull out of the ore eventually shut down the machine, the shift foreman angrily went to see what had caused the problem. Apparently all that was left of Lacey was his male organs. The poem ends, "The foreman said it was quite a sight by gawd, / and the guys on shift afterwards / used to wonder outloud about poor Lacey's wife" (11). Combined with rowdy speculation about Lacey and his wife's sexual relations is the question of how she is surviving without him, the larger reality of the mine worker's world.

These poems address the daily dangers of living and working in modern America, whatever one's cultural background. "To Change in a Good Way" is a narrative poem relating the friendship of a Laguna couple with an

Oklahoma couple. Bill, an "Okie," has come to Laguna to work in the mines. He and his wife Ida have no children, but they are very fond of Bill's younger brother, Slick, who is in Vietnam. One day at the mine, Bill gets a message from the foreman to call home, and he learns that Slick was killed when he stepped on an American land mine.

Bill's Laguna friend, Pete, brings Bill an ear of corn and a husk bundle, both ceremonial symbols of continuance. Bill places the bundle behind a rock in a mined-out stope and asks Slick's spirit to help them, "even if it's just so much as holding up / the roof of this mine that the damn company / don't put enough timbers and bolts in" (27). Ida will plant the corn the next spring. These Acoma people have shared their friendship and spirituality with the non-Native people who have come to live and work on their sacred land.

The Acoma attitude toward work as a sacred part of living is in stark contrast to the wage labor Acoma people have been forced into in more recent times. "Returning It Back, You Will Go On" says that the "land lets you" take from it, but the "only way the land will regenerate" is if you "give back" to the land, in the ancient way. One must work as respectfully with the land as the Acoma do in their tradition of nourishing the plants, not only by carefully preparing the ground but by watching, singing, and speaking about the plant "with compassion and love" (42). Well aware of the traditional respect for language among the Acoma, such as the language of traditional songs, Ortiz says, "My poems are prayers as well" (Sneve interview).

The essential caring for the land, for animals, and for humankind at the heart of Acoma culture is directly contradicted by the capitalist economic structure that exploits land and people for profit. *Fight Back* exposes the cunning technique the colonizers have used for hundreds of years, designed to make Native people blame themselves rather than the exploiters for their poverty and suffering. "No More Sacrifices" is the account of U.S. bureaucrats' reaction when Indian people demanded freedom for the thousand-year-old remains of a child that Americans had for many years displayed on postcards sold to tourists. The bureaucrats responded, "Indians were insensitive / to U.S. heritage" (49).

Ortiz also addresses American society's exploitation of Native culture for the purpose of presenting a falsely harmonious and positive view of history. His contemporary resistance follows the tradition of the Pueblo Revolt as he ends *Fight Back* and *Woven Stone* with "A New Story." When Ortiz was a patient at the V.A. hospital, a woman called to say she was looking for a "real Indian with feathers and paint" to ride on a float in the Frontier Day Parade. Later, when Ortiz was out of the hospital and teaching in a college, a different woman called with the same agenda—"she was looking for Indians" for a reenactment of Sir Francis Drake landing on the coast of California. The poem ends with this refusal: "'No,' I said. No" (*Woven Stone* 365). The resistance must begin with each Native person refusing to be trivialized, tokenized, or stereotyped, or to accept falsification of their history.

In his next book, *From Sand Creek* (1981), which received the Pushcart Prize for Poetry, Ortiz provides "an analysis of myself as an American, which is hemispheric, a U.S. citizen, which is national, and as an Indian, which is spiritual and human" (Preface). The book considers from these three perspectives the history and social environment surrounding a Veterans Administration hospital in Fort Lyons, Colorado. Again this book blends prose and poetry, and the format, like that of *Fight Back,* is a historical journey through greed and betrayal, with the Sand Creek Massacre as its central symbol. At Sand Creek, Colorado, Cheyenne leader Black Kettle and his band were attacked on November 29, 1864, by Fort Lyons troops and Colorado Volunteers under the command of Colonel John W. Chivington. A total of 105 women and children and 28 men were killed, despite the fact that they were peacefully camped under a U.S. flag that President Lincoln had presented to Black Kettle, with the promise that it would protect him and his band.

The poems of *From Sand Creek* chronicle the bleak truth of history that was acted out, both in massacres and in various schemes to deprive Native people of land and culture: "Whiskey was only one way and guns another . . . sell them anything, tell them it's for their own good" (48). But it was not just the Indians who fell victim to the relentless greed that has dominated America's history. Ortiz says that as Americans pushed westward, they swept "aside the potential / of dreams which could have been / generous and magnificent" (77), and that after this denial of dreams, Americans became "self-righteous and arrogant" (76). This coldness allowed them to deny any "regret / for the slaughter / of their future" (77).

From an Indian veteran's perspective, violence to the land and to the people is one. Yet, though blood is the central image of *From Sand Creek*, Ortiz's tone is ultimately hopeful: "The blood poured unto the plains, steaming like breath on winter mornings; the breath rose into the clouds and became the rain and replenishment" (66). Thus, the suffering of history can, when acknowledged, become part of a dream of America that is "wealthy with love" (95). Compassion is at the heart of the poems in this book, in which Ortiz considers the effects of colonization on both American Indians and people of European heritage. Like Elizabeth Cook-Lynn, Ortiz describes the historical enemies as those who have lusted for profits; and he carries this a step further, showing how those considered the heroes of American history have used and discarded not only land but people for monetary gain, ironically all in the name of God:

> Andrew Jackson claimed Him.
> He made his slave women bear
> his children for profit.
> And the fugitives crossed
> land and rivers
> and swept their trails clean
> forever from their memory.
> Their minds became technical
> and able and foresighted,
> looking towards Asia, Africa,
> the Mideast, Brazil. (91)

The poem indicates the loss of humanity that accompanies such a destruction of others. Living for the profits from other people's labor and for some new place to conquer requires an obliteration of the past, a denial of the bloody history of colonization. When Abenaki poet Joseph Bruchac asked him how history can be used in poems, Ortiz answered, "You have to use history. History is the experience we live. . . . We have to acknowledge that certain terrible things happened. If they don't want to say it, then we have to say it for them" (Bruchac 223); "we have to be revolutionary poets. Decolonization requires it." (227). Ortiz's favorite among the books he has authored, *From Sand Creek* was reissued at the beginning of the new century. The new edition is the same as the first, except for a longer preface, in which Ortiz reflects upon the place of Indian people in American history.

Ortiz's next book, *After and Before the Lightning* (1994), is set in a place distant from his Acoma home, near Okreek on the Rosebud Sioux Reservation in South Dakota. Its format is again that of a journey, although one more circumscribed than in earlier books. The vision of this journey is cosmic but tied to the season of winter, and the space he describes is as much sky as earth. In the preface he describes his feeling of "putting together a map of where I was in the cosmos" (xiv). Traveling Highway 18 from Mission to Okreek "feels like traveling on the farthest reaches of the galactic universe."

Having grown up in the desert Southwest, Ortiz was out of his element in South Dakota, yet his poetry about the winter experience on the northern prairie is insightful, filled with images of the beauty and power of the landscape. Awe and love fill the four parts of this book: "The Landscape: Prairie, Time, and Galaxy," "Common Trials: Every Day," "Buffalo Dawn Coming," and "Near and Evident Signs of Spring." These quarters are framed by poems about lightning, described in "Lightning II" as "dragon / sacred mysterious one" (n.p.).

Facing winter in South Dakota, Ortiz recognizes in "Earth Mother, She Cares" that "We can do nothing else / but pray, pray hard" (3). It is the earth, with her boiling blood, her shivering bones, that is powerful, and the experience of human helplessness in the face of such power makes one stand in awe.

In journal fashion, Ortiz dated many of the poems. "The Vision of Finework," dated December 5, is "Strata of snow, layers in a finework / only the wind has the skill to do" (37). In these lines, Ortiz reveals his own sensitivity to the source of Native art, which is nature's art.

Yet not all the poems are about the fulfillment of a spiritual or philosophical quest. In "Destination, Seeking," dated January 27, from the third section, Ortiz writes, "This morning's moon has only its significance. /

I cannot have the glow of its body for my own. / I only owe myself the humility of seeking it" (75).

"Prairie Night Song," dated February 22, is about the end of winter and the realization that has come from listening to its song: "The song of this night prairie curls softly, / deeply into a welcoming core of the spirit" (117).

The gentleness of these poems demonstrates the capacity of human beings in the modern moment to humbly look to the earth for spiritual insight. Ortiz speaks the language her songs teach. His honesty, compassion, and truth speak to the world.

Spirit Voices:

The

Poetry

of

Lance Henson

Chapter

5

With the verbal precision and conciseness that are characteristic of Native song, Lance Henson expresses a Cheyenne vision of the world. Henson is one of the few contemporary Native Americans writing poetry in both his indigenous language and English. His skill as a poet and his knowledge of Cheyenne language and culture have brought him national and international recognition. More than twenty collections of his poetry have been published, including seven published in Europe and translated into Italian, German, and Friesian. Henson has traveled widely, presenting many readings and workshops in Europe. He also has served as an official representative of the Southern Cheyenne Nation, addressing the European Free Alliance at Leeuwarden, the Netherlands, in 1985 and the Indigenous People's Conference at the United Nations in Geneva in 1988. He served the Southern Cheyennes in Geneva as a United Nations observer from 1997 through 1999. In 1999, he contacted many indigenous poets through their U.N. representatives for his project "Words from the Edge." The project brought together five poets whose peoples are endangered for a European reading tour from mid-October through mid–December 2000. Henson conceives of his poetry as "reflective of a globalized tribal vision."

Henson was born in Washington, D.C., September 20, 1944, but was raised near Calumet, Oklahoma (a community named for the *calumet,* or ceremonial pipe) by his great-aunt and uncle, Bertha and Bob Cook, whom he considers his grandparents. Bob Cook kept the grounds for Chapter Number One of the Native American Church in Oklahoma. Bertha Cook was a tipi maker. The last of five boys the couple raised, Henson is of Cheyenne, Oglala, and French ancestry, but he grew up living the Southern Cheyenne culture.

Upon graduation from Calumet High School, Henson joined the Marines during the Vietnam War. After serving in the military, he attended the Oklahoma College of Liberal Arts (now University of Science and Arts of Oklahoma) in Chickasha and began writing poetry. His first book, *Keeper of Arrows,* was published while he was a student in 1971. He graduated with a B.A. in English in 1972. From the fall of 1973 through the fall of 1974, Henson was a graduate student at the University of Tulsa. He has worked as a poet in schools throughout the United States and Europe. His poems have been included in the major anthologies of Native American literature and in a wide range of magazines, including *World Literature Today, National Geographic, Studies in American Indian Literatures,* and *Contact II.* Henson's national recognition as a poet includes being featured at the Geraldine R. Dodge Poetry Festival in New Jersey in 1992. Henson is a member of the Cheyenne Dog Soldier Society, the Native American Church, and the American Indian Movement.

Without capitalization, punctuation, or an extraneous word, Henson's poems create through heightened images the impressions and moods of

LANCE HENSON 67

historical places, people, and events. But he does not stop with the past. For Henson it is essential to interpret the significance of history's continuum into the present. Whether historical or contemporary, the people in his poetry interact with their place in dynamic and emotional relationships. The impressions his poems make are natural and subtle, like the fleeting perceptions that visit the mind. The reader's or hearer's response is more intuitive than rational. Henson's poetic voice and vision are defined in his September 27, 1991, statement at the Native American Writers' Forum in Telluride: "Indians are linked to metaphysical reality, live lives of heightened imagery, tell stories in images."

Some understanding of the history and culture of the Cheyennes is essential to comprehending Henson's poetry. By the nineteenth century, the Cheyennes were buffalo hunters who ranged over a vast territory. Their allies were the Lakota and Arapaho nations. By 1851, when the United States government's Horse Creek Treaty defined their territory as the area between the North Platte and Arkansas Rivers and stretching westward from the Ozarks into western Kansas and Nebraska, the Cheyenne were already splitting into Northern and Southern divisions, with the Northern Cheyenne living between the North Platte and the Yellowstone Rivers. The Southern Cheyenne became allied with the Arapaho, Kiowa, and Comanche. A portion of the Cheyenne who lived in Colorado were forced to accept a small reservation in the southeastern corner of that state in an 1861 treaty, but following the Civil War, white settlers were clamoring for that land, and the U.S. Cavalry under Colonel Chivington and Colorado volunteers joined forces to drive the Cheyenne out of the territory by an extermination policy. The most brutal attack on the Cheyenne was the Sand Creek Massacre of 1864.

By 1867, the U.S. government had decided to confine the Plains tribes to reservations. U.S. peace commissioners met with delegates of the Southern Cheyenne, Kiowa, Comanche, Plains Apache, and Southern Arapaho nations at Medicine Lodge in Kansas in 1867 and induced them to accept reservation lands. The army launched a series of campaigns to bring in the bands who refused to accept confinement. In 1868, the U.S. Cavalry under Colonel George Armstrong Custer attacked Black Kettle's Southern Cheyenne village, which was peacefully camped on the Washita River. Black Kettle, who had survived the Sand Creek Massacre, was killed, along with more than one hundred of his people and hundreds of Indian ponies.

Continued efforts by the government to reduce the territory of the Cheyenne and other nations of the southern plains resulted in the Red River War of 1874. In September of that year, at Palo Duro Canyon in Texas, Colonel Ranald Mackenzie attacked an encampment of Southern Cheyennes, Comanches, and Kiowas, burning four hundred lodges and slaughtering fourteen hundred ponies. The following winter, starving Indians drifted into the reservations from the plains. The completion of the first transcontinental railroad in 1869 and the near extinction of the buffalo that followed were forces even more powerful than massacres in forcing an end to the buffalo hunting life.

Following an executive order issued by President Ulysses S. Grant in 1869, the Cheyenne and Arapaho were restricted to a reservation in western Indian Territory in the spring of 1875. The U.S. government intended that they become farmer citizens, but many of the Cheyenne and Arapaho resisted acculturation and held to their traditional ways.

The first poem in Henson's first book, *Keeper of Arrows: Poems for the Cheyenne* (1971), introduced one of Henson's most prevalent poetic themes: the spiritual presence of those who have died. In "Morning" Henson describes steam from frost as "rising from the / backs of the / sleeping old" (n.p.), the bodies of his ancestors who had returned to the earth or of the animals who lived in earlier times. Variations of this theme appear throughout Henson's work but are particularly evident in Henson's early poetry. "Wherever I go I carry my relatives with me," Henson has said (University of South Dakota, October 12, 1978).

Henson developed this theme in *Naming the Dark: Poems for the Cheyenne* (1976), emphasizing that it is the spiritual essence to which all life tends. One of Henson's most moving and complete expressions of this theme is his poem "homecomings." While Henson was in the Marines, Bob Cook died. Two days before his death, Cook had mailed Henson some photographs he had taken of a March snowstorm in Oklahoma. When Henson returned to the Marine base after attending Cook's funeral, he found the photographs. In one of them, Cook was standing by the pumphouse at noon, with no shadow, only whiteness around him. In the final section of the poem, Henson speaks to the spirit of his relative, describing the photograph and its meaning: "you are in a photograph / standing in the snow / without a shadow / your words go into themselves / they reach a silent country where / we will meet / i have been going there forever" (15). Death, then, is the ultimate in homecomings; life, a progression toward one's spiritual home. The implication, reminiscent of Whitman, is that the only way we can be fully aware of life is to come to terms with the other "silent country," to accept that we are going there.

Henson even borrows Whitman's title, "Song of Myself," for one of the poems in this collection. Henson's "song of myself" is, like Whitman's, the individual expression of a poet who feels love for the place of his existence and who is in intimate touch with his environment: "there is a small light / like a whisper on the / leaves" (20). Though Henson writes in a far different style, the emotional, lyrical, and spiritual qualities of his poetry are similar to Whitman's.

In addition to personal poems, *Naming the Dark* also includes poems about the cultural heritage of the Cheyenne, such as "anniversary poem for the cheyennes who died at sand creek." Here Henson enters the experience of history through the place where peacefully camped Cheyenne people were massacred by cavalry forces in 1864. This poem expresses the belief that one can come close to the ghosts of the past by speaking "to the season / to the ponds / touching the dead grass" (21). One can learn by means beyond the stories and the history. The place itself has something to teach. As critic Robert L. Berner has observed, "Henson's best poems reveal a remarkable symbiosis of the personal and the traditional; they are the results of a process by which he receives power from his traditions while simultaneously enriching those traditions, helping them evolve, and ensuring their survival" (Berner 419).

Wild animals frequent Henson's poetry, carrying the traditional Cheyenne respect for coyote, owl, and badger into our modern time. Henson's third book is entitled *Mistah* (1978), the Cheyenne name for owl. Loneliness, emptiness, death, and silence fill the poems in this chapbook. The title poem is spoken through the voice of an owl "calling toward a house / in which / no one lives" (n.p.).

As Berner points out, the animals in Henson's poems are totemic, representative of their ancestors in Cheyenne tradition and legend. Bob Cook gave

Henson the Cheyenne name Mahago Domiuts, meaning Walking Badger, for a warrior ancestor who lived two hundred years earlier. Prefacing his interview with Henson in *Survival This Way* (1987), Joseph Bruchac says, "Like the badger he is capable of holding stubbornly to the things he believes in, even when confronted by those seemingly more powerful than he" (106). Explicating "song for warriors," in which Henson refers to the scent of the "carcass of badger" as "the blessing on my hands," Berner interprets the poem to mean that the badger's carcass "suggests a threat to the warrior ideal" (419). While this may be part of the meaning, the poem also suggests that finding this badger on the road, on a night after he has drunk "hours of beers at fats place," has brought the poet not only the feeling of "a deeper loss" but medicine, from the warriorlike badger brother with whom he identifies, to heal his spirit.

A small nation, the Southern Cheyenne have valued their language, which Henson learned from the Cooks as a child. Cheyenne words appear throughout his poetry, and he has written many bilingual poems. His book *This Small Sound/Dieser Kleine Klang* (1987), containing poems in English and Cheyenne with German translations, is one of a number of European editions of his poetry. The title of this collection is from Henson's "woodpecker song." The English version of the poem begins, "i am making this sound upon the earth." The Cheyenne words for this are *"hi do nah/na ma nist/sti doh/hist tah nov"* (28). Taking his cue as a poet from the woodpecker, Henson imitates this bird. Though small, the woodpecker uses his gifts perfectly, penetrating wood with his beak to obtain food. The tapping sound symbolizes his gift. The woodpecker is held sacred in the sun dance ceremony, in which the dancers aspire to be like the birds in the spirit of a strong and humble caring. The "small sound" of the woodpecker is concentrated, like Henson's poems. As Cherokee poet Gogisgi/Carroll Arnett said of Henson's poetry in an article for the *Dictionary of Native American Literature* (1994), "within that smallness is the concentration of spiritual energy" (446).

In the Native American world view, there is no separation between the various spheres of human life—spiritual, physical, political, emotional; all are one. The book *This Small Sound/Dieser Kleine Klang* contains "another song for america," which exemplifies Henson's growing concern with social issues.

The poem records Henson's response to driving "just past the kent state turnoff." He asks, "god damn you america / what have you done to your children" (31). The poem concludes, "the wind speaks their names / anyway you breathe it." The fact that the speaker is a Vietnam-era veteran intensifies the poem's impact. Henson shares with Simon Ortiz the conviction that the poet must condemn the crimes of American history. This would become the title poem of Henson's collection, *Another Song for America* (1987), in which Henson juxtaposes the modern and historical massacres. In "for white antelope," Henson includes the warrior's death song at Sand Creek—"nothing endures / only the earth and sky" (5). Berner has correctly observed that "Henson wants to suggest . . . that America's self-wounding at Kent State was an inevitable consequence of a history that has been written in the blood of his people" (420).

Henson has continuously expanded his vision and style. In the Winter 1993 issue of *American Indian Quarterly*, Craig Womack calls the poems in *Another Distance* (1991) "mini ceremonials that merge words, movement, and meaning and culminate in restored relationship and renewal" (108). Rena Cook, another of Henson's great-aunts, inspired the first two poems in the book. Her words in "poem from a master beadworker" go far beyond themselves, poignantly conveying the meaning of the creative act to an artist: "i close my eyes and bead in my head / and then i cry / i cry / and i guess my tears are the beads" (9). Out of Henson's minimalist style emerges a depth of emotion rare in literature. His natural way of expressing the cultural reality of the Southern Cheyennes through his own personal experience is what makes his poetry so unique and powerful.

A number of poems in *Another Distance,* including "a dream of european stones," written for Rena Cook, emerge from his travels in Europe. In poems written in Italy, Friesland, the Netherlands, Denmark, Sweden, Germany, Austria, and Luxembourg, Henson describes foreign landscapes from his Native American sensibility, finding precise metaphors that are at once metaphysical, geophysical, and emotional. In "two poems at elisabettas house," for example, he says, "my life is the dark sound / of someone walking on bruised stars / fallen to ground / as shards of stone / lit by the sun / and the seas tears" (12). Whether at home or abroad, the stones under one's feet are part of the creation, and life and the environment are composed of the same basic elements. Like Ortiz, Henson has written much of his best poetry about places far from his Native landscape.

Yet Henson remains Cheyenne in consciousness, and his roots in his culture and the land are nurtured by his return to Oklahoma each June for the sun dance. In an article published in *Oklahoma Today* (September–October 1993), journalist Maura McDermott quotes Henson as saying, "Western Oklahoma will always be my home" (49). Carrying on his family tradition, Henson's oldest son, Jon, also a poet, formed a drum group as a student at Fort Lewis College in Durango. A strong advocate for Native rights, Jon assisted his father's seventh Cheyenne sun dance in 1999.

Henson's "Journal Entries" in a 1991 issue of *Poetry East* indicate the direction his writing is taking. While similar in some ways to his early poetry, the lines are longer and their meanings more expansive: "there are ancestral horses underneath us warning us to be careful / with what is left / the dreaming horses echoing in the marrow of this land" (51). Conscious of our necessity to respect and protect the body of earth, if we are to survive, Henson includes himself in the collective *us*. The poem ends, "i lean back feeling my real name and close my eyes to the / pure and collective dark / that knows all our names" (52). Thus he has extended what he began to say in poems twenty years earlier, naming the "collective dark" and recognizing his connection to all of humanity.

The poems in *Strong Heart Song: Lines from a Revolutionary Text* (1997) were written during Henson's extensive travels through the United States and Europe from 1986 to 1994. With his bilingual title poem, "strong heart song," Henson sets this collection firmly in the tradition of Cheyenne culture and song. Yet the poems in this book also reflect modern life at the end of the twentieth century, in which journalists voted the bombing of Hiroshima and Nagasaki the most significant event of the century. In English, the poem says, "i will walk on the ashes of the earth / singing" (iii).

The poems that follow remember the history of America. An untitled poem written December 28, 1990, in memory of those who died a hundred years earlier, begins, "it is snowing tonight / on the barren plains at wounded knee" (3). The poem takes the reader to other places and peoples of North, Central, and South America. Evoking the "keening wind of winter" in which "there is a prayer," Henson ends in Cheyenne and English with "si vi wo ho oh shi win / we will not be thrown away" (3). This poem is a strong heart song showing the determination of Native people, like the descendants of those slaughtered at Wounded Knee and those still suffering in Guatemala and Nicaragua, to survive.

While Henson's poetry is rooted in traditional Cheyenne song, he acknowledges much broader influences, as in his poem "from a journal entry 9/18/86," which begins with a quote from the sixth-century Chinese poet Tu Fu that could be Henson's credo: "'the ideas of a poet should be noble and simple'" (4). The poem that follows highlights "the childs wide eyed stare" and "the moons thin arc" (4), images almost anyone can relate to. Although Henson's minimalist style is his own, he has traveled and read widely and acknowledges European, American, Spanish, Latin American, and Oriental literary influences. One can see especially in the brevity and imagery of his poems the influence of the haiku, a form that also influenced the poetry of contemporary Anishinabe writer Gerald Vizenor.

Some of the poems in *Strong Heart Song* are for poets—"dream of birds for roberta hill whiteman," "untitled for george trakl," "journal entry on a greyhound bus for maurice kenny," and "just after noon va alcohol recovery ward oklahoma city" (in which Henson thinks of Simon Ortiz and Carroll Arnett). Each honors the work of the poet named, as in these lines from his poem for Roberta Hill, who often uses internal rhyme in writing of nature's defiance of linear time: "a warm wind turns north / a woman falls into the heart of a flower / this is an hour standing apart" (36).

Henson's last lines in his *Strong Heart Song* are Cheyenne: "mahago do miutz / ehi woh" (73). Preceding them is this poetic statement: "the veho [white man's] world is crumbling / nothing made from ignorance / will remain" (73). These "lines from a revolutionary text III" indicate his belief that humanity can survive only through an awareness of our connection to nature.

Henson welcomed the new century in Switzerland, where he made his home for the final years of the twentieth century. Two books at the end of the century were published in bilingual English and German editions. *Revolutionslied,* published in 1998, confirms Henson's earlier poetic statements that revolution is epitomized in the natural world. In "revolutionary song," written January 31, 1997, in Milan, Henson asks,

is it a river or a breeze
or the running water that grieves
onto itself
that makes one wish to be free

The final lines of this poem answer his question:

on a morning of frost
in the soreness of waking
the cry of humanity goes out of itself
as impossible to stop
as the weeping of water
as the weeping of a child

Yes, Henson answers, there is a continuing cry against injustice, a cry that runs deep in the consciousness of nature and humanity everywhere.

Lieder in der Sprache des Feindes/Songs in the Enemy's Language (1999) features Henson's poetry juxtaposed with paintings by Swiss artist Lisa Schnorf. The poems in this book are in three parts: "visitations/heimsuchungen," "signature of dusk/zeichen der dammerung," and "twelve songs in the enemy's language/zwolf lieder in der sprache des feindes." Henson's "visitations" recall scenes and people, relating them to his present life. The poet's consciousness spans time and space. In a poem written in Lafarre, France, under the "peyote moon," he speaks a prayer in the Cheyenne language: "aho maheo na shivadom ni nisha / (creator bless my granddaughter)" (24). Thinking of earlier poets, he writes in "ginsberg sonata," "allen has gone underground / into the incomprehensible landscape of america / . . . / he stands now smoking cigars / with whitman under a canopy in the rain" (34).

Desolate postcolonial images fill the poems of "the signature of dusk." In "observations from the third world," Henson writes,

deep in the rain forest in brazil
the yanomami women are selling their bodies
as prostitutes
so their warriors
can afford guns and ammunition
to fight the gold miners (46)

There is additional social commentary in this poem written in Biver, France, January 23, 1995, as he thinks of other prostitutes as two ravens sent into the flooded world by Noah:

I met them in the red light district in amsterdam
last year
disguised as defrocked monks
I told them I was flying toward america
they told me they were still flying away
from the ark . . . (48)

The "twelve songs in the enemy's language," which end the book, are spoken from the perspective of a traditional Cheyenne. While they are written in English and translated into German, both the enemy's language, they remember Sand Creek, Little Fingernail, and other places and people familiar to the Cheyenne people. These poems resonate with the deep respect for the cosmos that is characteristic of Henson's poetry. Beginning with the Cheyenne words "wo he iv / do sah ni vistoh," the final song asks, "morning star / what do you see" (98).

An Instrument for Song:

The Poetry

of

Roberta Hill

Chapter
6

There could be no more perfect metaphor for the poetry of Roberta Hill than the title image of her first book, *Star Quilt* (1984). Each of her poems is as carefully crafted and as richly evocative as the symbolism in a star quilt. In an interview, Hill told Joseph Bruchac that writing the poem "Star Quilt" helped her to conceive of writing poetry as a process with a purpose, "as making something—like a quilt . . . it can be used for something . . . the quilt made . . . . for a fast or a guest helps that person" (Bruchac, *Survival* 326). The star quilt metaphor links Hill to a community of women artists, since the star quilt is a useful form of art made by contemporary Native American women. In her poem, Hill asks the quilt to "anoint us with grass and twilight air, / so we may embrace, two bitter roots / pushing back into the dust" (1): the apparent goal of her poetry. Hill seeks to nurture us in a hard and bitter time. Like all of her work, "Star Quilt" unfolds within a carefully crafted pattern. Of the seven three-line clusters, some are end stopped; others, enjambed. Alliteration is frequent. And the stanzas are filled with images of light:

These are notes to lightning in my bedroom.
A star forged from linen thread and patches.
Purple, yellow, red like diamond suckers, children
of the star gleam on sweaty nights. The quilt unfolds
against sheets, moving, warm clouds of Chinook.
It covers my cuts, my red birch clusters under pine. (1)

The juxtaposition of images from nature with others from ordinary domestic life in "Star Quilt" is characteristic of Hill's poetry. The quilt functions like a warm Chinook wind, literally and figuratively protecting the ones it covers.

Through synesthetic and impressionistic language, Hill fills her poetry with spiritual implications, as in these lines from "Winter Burn":

When birds break open the sky, a smell of snow
blossoms on the wind. You sleep, wrapped up
in blue dim light, like a distant leaf of sage. (*Star Quilt* 31)

The Native Americans in Hill's poems have an attitude of dignified acceptance. No matter how they have conducted their lives, they have within them a sense of wonder at the magnificent experience of life. They respect the creation. As Carolyn Forche states in the foreword to *Star Quilt*, "One finds in this work a map of the journey each of us must complete . . . as children and exiles of the Americas. So there is a spiritual guidance here, uncommon in contemporary letters" (ix).

A member of the Oneida Nation, Hill grew up near Green Bay and Oneida, Wisconsin. Her paternal grandmother, Dr. Lillie Rosa Minoka Hill, loved to recite poetry to her children and grandchildren. Hill recalls, "I remember . . . sitting in her lap and listening to her tell stories. . . . She left us . . . some of the very few books that we had and they were poetry, Wordsworth and Shakespeare . . . as a child that was my favorite pastime, sitting underneath the dining room table and trying to wade through the books" (Bruchac, *Survival* 327).

When Hill was young, her mother Eleanor Hill died of liver cancer; and that loss, Hill says, "led me to a real awareness of life" (327). Her father Charles Allen Hill was a teacher and musician, and Hill credits him with her love of language and rhythm (327). She had written in journals from childhood, and even though her father had encouraged her to study science in college, she majored in creative writing and psychology at the University of Wisconsin, then went on to study creative writing with Richard Hugo at the University of Montana, where she completed her M.F.A. in 1973.

Some of Hill's earliest poems were published in *Carriers of the Dream Wheel* (1975). Her poetry has appeared in most subsequent anthologies of

Native American poetry and in such magazines and anthologies as *The American Poetry Review, The Nation, The Third Woman,* and *Reinventing the Enemy's Language.* She has written two books of poetry, *Star Quilt* (1984) and *Philadelphia Flowers* (1996).

Hill has read her poetry throughout the United States, in mainland China, and in Canada. She has been a poet-in-the-schools in Minnesota, Arizona, Wyoming, South Dakota, Oklahoma, Montana, and Wisconsin. She has taught creative writing on the Oneida Reservation in Wisconsin, on the Rosebud Reservation in South Dakota, and at the University of Wisconsin in Madison and Eau Claire.

In 1980, Hill married Ernest Whiteman, an Arapaho artist. He and their children, Jacob, Heather, and Melissa, are featured in her poetry. She has published most of her poetry under the name Roberta Hill Whiteman; however, after the two divorced in 1996, Hill resumed her original name.

In 1997, Hill became director of the American Indian Studies Program at the University of Wisconsin in Madison. She completed a Ph.D. in American studies at the University of Minnesota in 1998. Her dissertation, "Dr. L. Rosa Minoka Hill and her 'Inconspicuous Way,'" won a Native American Prose Award from the University of Nebraska Press in 1998. Holy Cow! Press published a fifteenth-year anniversary edition of her book *Star Quilt* in 1999.

Arranged in four seasons, *Star Quilt* moves from fall ("Sometimes in Other Autumns") to winter ("' . . . Fighting Back the Cold with Tongues'") to spring ("Love, the Final Healer") to summer ("Music for Two Guitars").

One of the strongest poems in the autumn season is "Leap in the Dark," which offers a woman's perspective on the house, work, nature, food, present and past that surround her: "When the sun opened clouds and walked into her mongrel soul, / she chopped celery into rocky remnants of the sea. . . . / The magnet in each seed of the green pepper kept her flying, / floating toward memories that throb like clustered stars" (14). With reference to this poem, Paula Gunn Allen has perceptively remarked that Hill's poetry exemplifies the theme of reconciliation, and that she is one of the poets who have negotiated "the perilous path between life and death, between bonding and dissolution, between tribal consciousness and modern alienation" by means of the "transformational metaphor" (*Sacred Hoop* 161–62).

Hill's transformational metaphors are often facets of the traditional life of the Oneida. For example, another autumn poem, "In the Longhouse, Oneida Museum," begins with the line "House of five fires, you never raised me." The poem describes her house of youth as "a shell of sobs," yet it ends in an affirmation of Hill's connection to traditional Oneida life:

> House of five fires, they take you for a tomb,
> but I know better. When desolation comes,
> I'll hide your ridgepole in my spine
> and melt into crow call, reminding my children
> that spiders near your door
> joined all the reddening blades of grass
> without oil, hasp or uranium. (16, 17)

The *Haudenausaunee,* or People of the Longhouse, as the Oneida refer to themselves, trace their origins to what is now central New York state. By the sixteenth century they had joined with four other nations, the Cayuga, Mohawk, Onondaga, and Seneca, to form the Iroquois League for peace. In 1714, the Tuscarora joined the other five, and the alliance became the Iroquois League of Six Nations.

The democratic principles of the Iroquois League and other indigenous cultures and the spirit of freedom in the Americas influenced the revolutionary fervor for liberation from colonial rule and America's new form of government. Benjamin Franklin and more recently Suzan Shown Harjo and Bruce Johansen have pointed out that Native Americans deserve substantial credit for this new way of thinking.

During the American Revolution, the Oneida and Tuscarora remained neutral, while the other four nations fought alongside the British. When George Washington's troops were starving at Valley Forge, the Oneida gave them corn. Yet the U.S. government later allowed land speculators to defraud the Oneida of their land. Early in the nineteenth century, Eleazer Williams, an Episcopalian missionary, persuaded the Oneidas to move west. He and several Oneida chiefs went to see the land of the Menominees and HoChungra near Green Bay, Wisconsin, and the Oneida bought land from the Menominees in 1822. The federal government eventually recognized the land in Wisconsin as their reservation; nevertheless, the Oneida continue to identify with their original homeland, and their title to that territory in central New York is still being litigated. Hill's poetry emerges from the history of her people's dispossession from their original homeland and forced resettlement.

Her poetry also embraces the experience of other Native cultures, such as the Lakota. "Reaching Yellow River," from the winter season of *Star Quilt*, is almost entirely a monologue from the perspective of a Lakota man, Mato Heholgeca's (Hollow-horned Bear's) grandson, in whose memory the poem was written. Imagining the last binge before the death of an alcoholic, the poem is witty and poignant: "For six days / I raced Jack Daniels. / He cheated, told jokes. / Some weren't even funny. / That's how come he won" (26). Nevertheless, at the end, the young Lakota man is united with nature: "Foxtails beat / the grimace from my brow / until I took off my pain / like a pair of old boots. / I became a hollow horn filled / with rain, reflecting everything" (27–28). At the end, Mato Heholgeca nudges his grandson as he calls out his Lakota name; but his grandson has died, in an ironic reversal of human longevity.

"Beginning the Year at Rosebud, S.D.," another winter poem, describes life on the reservation in unrelenting graphic images: "Raw bones bend from an amber flood of gravel, / used clothing, whiskey. We walked, and a dead dog / seemed to leap from an iced shore, barks swelling her belly" (30). But life on the reservation is not entirely bleak. There are historical memories there that can be found nowhere else: "A withered grandmother's face trickles wisdom / of buffalo wallows and graveyards marked with clumps of sage" (30). Yet the poem ends in sadness: "I know of a lodestone in the prairie, / where children are unconsoled by wishes, / where tears salt bread" (30). Winter is hard on a South Dakota reservation, and Hill's early poems express this reality, foreshadowing the development of a similar perspective in the poetry of Sherman Alexie.

The spring season of *Star Quilt* centers on love. One of the spring poems, "An Old Man's Round for the Geese," is written in four-line ballad stanzas and, as the traditional English ballad often does, laments failed love. The old man identifies with the migrating geese: "I know why the wild goose flies, / the blood in its veins is burning. / I know why the wild goose flies, / filled with incredible yearning" (46). Though like the geese he may have followed the urge to travel, he can't fly like them, nor has his love been so constant or permanent as theirs. The poem ends: "I wasn't as lucky as the geese / that meet to love a lifetime. / I wasn't as lucky as the geese / Bring me more wine, more wine" (46).

Several spring poems are addressed to or concern Hill's family members. "For Heather, Entering Kindergarten" expresses a mother's fears that in school her daughter will be taught to discard her Indian heritage: "I'm afraid / she'll learn the true length of forlorn, / the quotient of the Quick / who claim that snowflakes never speak, / that myths are simply lies" (54). "Minor Invasions" recalls the sometimes monotonous and miserable life of Hill's mother, a nurse, who often worked too hard at trying to have a model 1950s home: "Dust knows the value of lost days, / days when do, do, do wrenches / from us the screech of boxcars" (57). A mother tries to teach her son to accept his life in "Love, the Final Healer": "Scared and hot, you fussed for hours / in the light of a motel, / . . . / We're caught in some old story. / I'm the woman winter loved / and you, the son of winter, ask / where did he go and why. / This poem gets cut to just one sentence: / You grow old enough and I get wise" (59). The poem ends in an affirmation of love: "After every turn of innocence and loss, / . . . / when we give what's true and deep, / . . . / love, the final healer, makes certain / that we grow. A bug, a bird, a phrase from some old story or a friend will find us. / Then we'll remember winter as a cleansing." (59). These poems suggest that being aware of one's relationships not only to other human beings but to the entire cycle of history and the environment is essential to wellness and growth.

Recalling Lance Henson's observation about the origin of thoughts, "'When you're walking on the earth, they come up through your feet'" (Bruchac, *Survival* 334), led Hill to think of Oneida women dancing in the traditional way: "When you dance . . . you massage the earth. And I like to think of that connection, that the earth is telling us things" (334). "Woman Seed Player," dedicated to Yanktonai Sioux artist Oscar Howe, describes a painting that brought Hill encouragement: "She doesn't force the day / to fit her expectations. / Now she pulls me through" (74). The theme of this summer section, and an important concept in Hill's poetry, is that it is essential in life and in art to allow oneself to be influenced by nature, rather than to attempt to control it.

Hill conceives of herself as an instrument through which poetry is written. "Music for Two Guitars," the title poem of the summer season, is dedicated to her husband, Ernie Whiteman. Choosing guitars as metaphors for this man and herself, she writes, "You have robbed my hesitation and distrust. / You have taken my fears and wrapped them in fires. / Full of possibilities, I cannot name what rings me. / Bell or empty bowl? Guitars on the verge of song" (63). Life, then, plays the poet, who offers the world the music of words.

Nature's music is transformational in Hill's "Conversation Overheard on Tamalpais Road" from Dexter Fisher's anthology *The Third Woman* (1980). The dialogue is between two women, Barnarda, crippled in a wheelchair, and her sister, who asks, "Aren't you bitter?" Barnarda's answer reveals wisdom and spirituality that allow her to transcend her physical state. Though the former flamenco dancer can no longer dance "in the stomp sting of stepping / to the music of guitars" (125), she now has come to the understanding "that we are most alive when letting go." Barnarda says, "I dance on, gladdened / by a purling world. Can your guarded eyes / believe this reach of wind, this transparent sea?" (125). There is a quiet dignity in the voice of Barnarda and in that of Roberta Hill, a firm footing that acknowledges the source of human life and stands in awe of its great spiritual possibilities.

Hill's second book, *Philadelphia Flowers* (1996), comprises two groups of poems, each beginning with a reference to "The Traditional History of the Confederacy of the Six Nations." The first poem states her purpose, which coincides with that of the Iroquois creator: "to bring comfort and care" (9). This is a humble yet essential aspiration for a troubled time. In "Kalanchoe," the second poem, she says to the plant, "Heal me, lovely, burning / so green, like jade stones / the old ones placed in the mouths / of their dead" (11). The poem recognizes the reciprocal nurturing of a plant for its caretaker, who comes to understand through observing her houseplant her own need to flower.

The poems in this collection extend beyond the domestic domain to address the broader spheres of American history and society. For example, in "Where I Come From," Hill refutes the anthropological assumption that the natives of North America came from Asia, saying, "I come from the red earth of Turtle Island. / This earth has always been our home. / My ancestors were not immigrants from Asia" (17). The style of these poems, with their direct declarations in separate lines, is far different from that of Hill's more psychological, imagistic, and grammatically complex earlier poems. Instead, these poems confront contemporary political realities.

"Acknowledgment" asks North American readers to accept some responsibility for the suffering and death of the people of Latin America: "Listen, for the Lord / of the Near and Close comes / to make you see / in steam rising from coffee, smoke from bodies burning in Panzos. / Sometime he'll have you taste / in your chocolate bars / that bitterness children carry / when they dare not bury / their bludgeoned mothers" (22). This poem powerfully connects the consumption of coffee, chocolate, flowers, and sugar to the suffering of the people whose labor is exploited produce these products and profits for their oppressors. Hill asks: "Will you acknowledge the love / and faith of our restless earth, / or will you claim the suffering's / too far south while your mouth / samples and measures, calls everything / tangible?" (23).

The second part of the book begins with a statement made centuries ago to the tyrant Tha-do-dah-ho, who was Onondaga, by the Peacemaker, Dekanawida, who was probably Huron: "'These Lords who now stand all around you have now accepted the good tidings of Peace and Power, which signifies that now hereafter the shedding of human blood shall cease, for our Creator, the Great Spirit, never intended that man should engage in any such work of destruction of human life.'" (57). But unfortunately, the people living on Turtle Island have yet to shun destruction and live together in peace.

The title poem, "Philadelphia Flowers," describes a homeless woman sleeping in the entrance of a city building. Juxtaposed with contemporary scenes of urban blight are tribal memories of the Iroquois sachems who explained to the founders of Pennsylvania that "the law that kept them unified / required a way to share the wealth" (60). But this city, a cradle of the new democracy, has not kept its promise to the poor. The first section of this four-part poem ends, "Our leaders left this woman in the lurch. / How can there be democracy / without the means to live?" (60).

The second section is about the violence that is part of contemporary urban life. Confusion over the cause of a mattress fire leads the police to storm a group of Mohawk ironworkers whom they falsely assume are rioting. Terrified, the men fight back, and one of them is shot and dragged down four flights of stairs by the police. Based on a true incident, the poem indicts the often brutal police treatment of Native Americans and other minorities.

In the third section, a Mohawk woman is passing through the city, "tracking my Mohawk grandmother," when someone "tall, dark, intense / with a bun of black hair and the gaze of an orphan" stops her, "shoving flowers toward my arm" (63): "'At least, I'm not begging,'" the person cries. At the center of the poem is the desperate need to keep a measure of pride by supporting oneself. The poet compares herself to the person selling a mixture of wild and cultivated flowers—"iris, ageratum, goldenrod and lilies"(63) and wishes she had bought more of those "Philadelphia flowers."

The fourth section describes the planned exploitation of the forests and land: "Next they'll want the water and the air" (64). Hill's warning, "they're planning to leave our reservations bare of life. They plan to dump their toxic / wastes on our grandchildren," is based on realities, such as the attempts of various states, including Minnesota, to send the waste products of nuclear power plants to be buried on Indian reservations. These are the fruits of a society that shirks its responsibility for the people as a whole, but that allows individuals with the power of wealth to deprive many others of the basic necessities. The poem ends with a warning to all: "What of you, learning how this continent's / getting angry? Do you consider what's in store for you?" Philadelphia seems a long way from the reservation, but even large cities like Philadelphia were once the domain of the Indians.

Despite their seeming invisibility in this modern society, poets such as Hill affirm the identity and place of indigenous people. In "The Powwow Crowd," Hill shows many parallels between Indians dancing and the world surrounding them: "Familiar elements dance. Soil / and water, fire, rock and air" (115). "Plants taught us to dance," she says, and "Planets also powwow." The dancing, then, is a reflection of cosmic life, from the tiny atom to the blazing sun. Though spectators at a powwow may see only a social gathering, the dancing, like other forms of indigenous art, including poetry, is in truth a reenactment essential to the continuance of life on the planet.

Translating the World:

The Poetry

of

Linda

Hogan

Chapter

7

Linda Hogan's writing examines people's essential relationship to land, to animals, and to one another from a traditionally minded Chickasaw perspective. She recognizes the precariousness and complexity of these relationships at the turn of the century. Believing that "Everything speaks," Hogan says that her job as a poet is to "listen to the world and translate it into a human tongue" (Coltelli 72). Her imagination and politics are informed by Chickasaw tradition, by living close to the earth, and by the working- and poverty-class life of her childhood. Her poetry has evolved from a culturally specific perspective to include a universal consideration of human relationships and responsibilities to place and to others.

Born in Denver to Cleona Bower Henderson and Charles Henderson, Linda Henderson Hogan lived part of her childhood in Colorado Springs and part in Germany, where her father was stationed in the army. Her family maintained close ties with relatives in Oklahoma, where Linda spent summers with her grandparents, who lived on Chickasaw allotment and then relocation land near Gene Autry.

Hogan has stated that there were no books in her home, except for the Bible; but stories told by her father and uncle were a literary resource that later enriched her writing (Autobiographical statement 78). Hogan's great-grandmother Addie was a granddaughter of Winchester Colbert, head of the Chickasaw Nation. She married Granville Walker Young, a rancher and politician of Metis ancestry. Their daughter, Lucy Young, was Hogan's grandmother. Lucy graduated from Bloomfield Academy for Chickasaw Girls in 1904. She then married a Chickasaw, Charles Colbert Henderson, and her father disowned her. Hogan remembers that when she was a child, these grandparents had no water, electricity, or plumbing (Swann and Krupat 236–38).

Hogan's poetry also includes references to her mother's immigrant family, who had settled in Nebraska. This mixed ancestry "created a natural tension that surfaces in my work and strengthens it" (Coltelli 71). Hogan's great-grandfather, W. E. Bower, hoed broom corn and hauled wood for a railroad before homesteading in Nebraska in 1872. In a desperate struggle to survive, he also hunted buffalo, beaver, and antelope (Swann and Krupat 234).

Hogan left the land of her ancestors in her late teens and moved to California, where she worked as a nurse's aide and later began adult education classes. Years later she moved to Maryland, outside of Washington, D.C., where she began to write poetry (Bruchac, *Survival* 121). She completed a bachelor's degree in English at the University of Colorado at Colorado Springs and went on to complete an M.A. in English and creative writing at the University of Colorado in 1978. Hogan has been poet-in-residence for the Colorado and Oklahoma Arts Councils. She has taught at Colorado College, Colorado Women's College, the University of Minnesota, and the University of Colorado at Boulder. In her lectures, readings, and workshops at universities, in Native communities, and at conferences throughout the United States, Hogan urges her audiences and students to consider the impact of racism, classism, and other forms of oppression. An avid reader, Hogan wants "to keep a finger on the pulse of the whole world" (Coltelli 83). She cites as influences poets Pablo Neruda and Elizabeth Bishop, N. Scott Momaday's novel *House Made of Dawn*, and many works in translation. However, she places literary influences in the same category as "trees, weather, dreams, insects, sun."

Among her many fellowships and awards are an American Book Award from the Before Columbus Foundation for *Seeing Through the Sun* (1985), a Yaddo Artists Colony Residency Fellowship, a D'Arcy McNickle Memorial Fellowship, a John Simon Guggenheim fellowship, a Lannan Foundation Award in poetry, a National Endowment for the Arts grant in fiction, and the Five Tribes Museum Play Writing Award. Her essays and short stories have been published widely in such magazines as *Prairie Schooner, Denver Quarterly, The Greenfield Review, Ms.*, and *Parabola*. Currently, Hogan is working for the Chickasaw Nation as editor of the *Journal of Chickasaw History* and living and writing in Idledale, Colorado.

Hogan's early poems in *Calling Myself Home* are filled with the stark imagery of the Oklahoma landscape and more obviously rooted in Chickasaw tradition than much of her later work. The movement of Hogan's family during her childhood, from Denver to Oklahoma and back, was similar in some ways to the earlier movements of her Chickasaw ancestors. Among the "five civilized tribes" forced to move on the Trail of Tears, the Chickasaw left their homes in the southeastern United States in the 1830s for Indian Territory, which would become Oklahoma by the end of the nineteenth century.

The Chickasaw had earlier lived in a vast territory bounded on the north by the Ohio River, on the south by the Gulf of Mexico, and on the west by the Mississippi River (Gibson 3–4). These land boundaries varied over time as a result of the sometimes migratory lifestyle of the tribe of hunters and agriculturists.

According to a Chickasaw legend, the nation's search for a home began at an ancient time, when the tribe lived in the West. As they traveled, they carried with them a pole, which spiritual leaders placed upright in the ground at their campsite. During the night the pole moved about, and the direction it had assumed by morning served as a compass to guide that day's travel. Almost always it pointed east. The Chickasaw kept moving eastward until they arrived at the Tennessee River. The following morning the pole was erect, directing them to settle there. With great rejoicing they cleared the land, planted corn, and built villages. Spiritual leaders kept watch over the sacred pole, which in time leaned westward. The Chickasaw then abandoned their villages and moved westward to the highlands of northeastern Mississippi, where the pole again remained erect. Thus the people settled there (Gibson 10–11). The spirit of place, in the form of prevailing winds, was seen by the Chickasaw as a guiding power, which they respected and followed. Hogan refers to this tradition in the last stanza of her poem "Heritage," which recalls the words of her grandmother: "She told me how our tribe has always followed a stick / that pointed west / that pointed east" (*Calling Myself Home* 17). Migration patterns undertaken willingly by the Chickasaw Nation were contradicted by their nineteenth-century forced removal from the Southeast by the Andrew Jackson administration. This injustice forged Hogan's ironic statement at the end of "Heritage": "From my family I have learned the secrets / of never having a home" (17).

The transience that has been part of Hogan's personal and tribal past may have influenced her ability to extend her identification with place beyond the boundaries of a particular locale. When once asked if specific places are important to her, and what she meant by her title *Calling Myself Home*, she said, "Oklahoma is my first place. It is my early memories. It created me. . . . *Calling Myself Home* has to do with returning to and remembering home, Oklahoma, in my case. It also has to do with being at home in this body and self, coming to terms with change, moves, with life" (Wilson, "Turtles" 7).

The turtle, the animal that appears most frequently in her early poems, represents Hogan herself and the Chickasaw people. From Hogan's childhood came the memory of women dancing with turtleshell rattles on their legs in Chickasaw healing dances and ceremonials. The poem "turtle," which opens *Calling Myself Home,* celebrates the relationship between women and the generative power of turtles: "we are women. / The shells are on our backs. / We are amber, / the small animals / are gold inside us" (3). Commenting on this and other poems in Hogan's first book, Andrew Wiget says, "In the languid rhythms of dream speech and the discontinuity of associated images, she suggests the transformation of persons not only into animals but into aspects of the earth such as trees, clay and sedimentary rock" (119). Such transformations suggest an investment of body and spirit in the entire creation.

In the Chickasaw Picofa ceremony, medicine people fast for three days before administering remedies to a seriously ill person. On the third day men and women of the patient's clan gather to dance and sing. The women wear turtleshell rattles in this ceremony (Gibson 15). Even after their removal to Indian Territory, the Chickasaw continued this healing ceremony, recalled in the title poem "Calling Myself Home," when old women lace together the shells of turtles after placing pebbles inside them and dance "with rattles strong on their legs" (6). Urging women of her own generation to awaken to their inheritance, Hogan suggests that women have the strength to sustain and preserve the earth: "The land is the house / we have always lived in. / The women, / their bones are holding up the earth."

Celebrating the regeneration of life and the relationships that are embodied in the female cycle in "Celebration: Birth of a Colt," Hogan recalls watching a mare, Lady, give birth. The images are precise, the experience unified and complete, as the mare licks her colt to its feet and the "sun coming up shines through" (13) the "red, transparent" membrane of afterbirth. Extending red imagery, "the sky turns bright with morning / and the land / everywhere it is red," Hogan makes visible the interrelatedness of the colt, the sky, the land, and the red people. These early poems, along with several short stories, were republished in *Red Clay* (1991).

An important facet of woman's relationship to the earth is her relationship to the life that she nurtures. Hogan's daughters, Sandra and Tanya, have inspired her work. The mother–child, particularly the mother–daughter relationship is central to Hogan's poetry. Her second book is *Daughters, I Love You* (1981), which she included as a section of her third book, *Eclipse*

(1983). Hogan presents the mother–daughter relationship as tender, yet painful for the mother, who is unable to protect her daughter from suffering and who must finally be separate from the daughter whom she holds dear. In *Daughters, I Love You,* Hogan laments the exploitation and danger imposed on nature by the concept, alien to Native Americans, that land is a commodity which individual humans can own. There are few direct references to Chickasaw tradition in this collection, which was an outgrowth of Hogan's experience at the 1980 International Survival Gathering, held near the Black Hills of South Dakota. Hogan was among the thousands of people who camped at the week-long Survival Gathering on Marvin Kammerer's ranch, adjacent to Ellsworth Air Force Base, to protest nuclear development. These poems grew from the seeds of a vision evident in her first book, directed at what is not seen with the eye but nonetheless present—"gold atoms dancing underground" (*Calling Myself Home* 6). In an interview with Native American poet and critic Paula Allen, Hogan said, "I feel that what people are doing from the very beginning of the mining process all the way to the final explosion is that they're taking a power out of the earth that belongs to the earth. They're taking the heart and soul of the earth" (168–69).

Hogan's confrontation with nuclear power is both personal and global. In the first poem, "Daybreak," her daughter is compared to all the children of the earth whose innocence is threatened by war, to those who have been and remain its victims: "In her dark eyes / the children of Hiroshima / are screaming" (*Daughters, I Love You* n.p.). But the poem is not just about suffering. Hogan reminds us that it is because "it is a good thing to be alive / and safe / and loving every small thing" that we must grieve when life is threatened. Hogan seeks to exert the generative power of language against the destructive power that endangers all innocent and loving people. Wiget calls the poems in this book "more protest than plea" and notes that they "exploit ironies of transformation" (119). Certainly, nuclear war reverses the nurturing capacity of the atom and of women and the earth, destroying the balance and order of nature. Camped at the end of the runway, constantly assaulted by the roar of B-52's, people at the gathering were like all of Earth's inhabitants, at "ground zero / in the center of light" with bombs "buried beneath us" and "destruction" flying over our heads. Yet "Black Hills Survival Gathering, 1980" ends in "Radiant morning" with images of Buddhist monks "singing and drumming / Heartbeat." Paula Allen says of Hogan, "Being an Indian enables her to resolve the conflict that presently divides the non-Indian feminist community; she does not have to choose between spirituality and political commitment, for each is the complement of the other. They are the two wings of one bird, and that bird is the interconnectedness of everything" (169).

The working-class perspective and sense of irony and humor so important in Hogan's work are apparent in "Oil," from her book *Eclipse*. The people, "full of bread and gas," grow "fat on the outside / while inside we grow thin"(11). Self-deprecating humor helps to sustain these workers, but the injuries inflicted on them and on the earth by the greed that fuels our consumer society may, Hogan implies, be irreversible: "The earth is wounded / and will not heal" (11).

Human greed has so perverted our natural reciprocal relationship with the environment that children are starving in regions that could produce an abundance of food. The title poem of Hogan's book *Seeing Through the Sun* (1985) refers to the violence, poverty, and danger that people who live in the repressive, militaristic societies of Latin America and other regions face each day, through a series of related symbolist images: "In that country of light / there is no supper / though the sun's marketplace / reveals . . . / burning round oranges, / wheat loaves, / and the men's uniforms with shining buttons" (3).

Always speaking out for human freedom, Hogan attempts to mirror the complex and often oppressive reality that, when seen, should incite us to act. In "Folksong," she parallels the experience of the Latvians, whose nation was controlled by the Soviet Union, to that of the Chickasaw, controlled by the U.S. government since the early nineteenth century. When men have the power to "change the living / to the dead," she says, "Even the hungry take to politics" (8). Countering the destructive use of language exerted by the men in power are the "sweet songs of sparrows" and the folksongs of the native people.

Hogan includes in "Wall Songs" the history of her own and her

Chickasaw ancestors' suffering as a result of the racial/cultural barrier: "There is a song / chanting from out of the past, / voices of my evicted grandmothers / walking a death song / wrapped in trade cloth / out of Mississippi" (67). The trade cloth seems to symbolize Hogan's mixed identity: born between cultures, Hogan writes, "Open the cloth / and I fall out" (67). The other song in the poem is her grandfather's "No Whites May Enter Here" (67), which created, Hogan says, a barrier of racial prejudice, "the confines of this flesh." The poem ends with a prayer for an end to all the artificial barriers separating human beings from one another and from nature.

"I think of my work as part of the history of our tribe and as part of the history of colonization everywhere," Hogan has written (Swann and Krupat 233). Not satisfied with conveying history, Hogan attempts to shape history with her poems as she consciously identifies, not only with her own Chickasaw culture but with all colonized people. Hogan finds deep, archetypal images to exert the power of language in shaping her historical vision. In "To Light," she writes, "Even the trees with their rings / have kept track / of the crimes that live within / and against us" (197).

Hogan's essay "Who Puts Together" deals with the power of language to "function as a poetic process of creation, transformation, and restoration" (103): "As energy, language contains the potential to restore us to a unity with earth and the rest of the universe" (112). But in order for this to occur, words must be used with creative care. The process that leads to unity is often recorded in Hogan's poems. In "The New Apartment, Minneapolis," from her book *Savings* (1988), she describes a house in which "floorboards creak" and "burns remain / on the floor" (9). Thinking of the Indian tenants before her, she chronicles the continued brutality of whites: "last spring white merchants hung an elder / on a meat hook and beat him" (9). She looks "through the walls of the houses" at the variety of people living there—"baking," or "sleeping" or "getting drunk" or "crying or making jokes" or "laughing" (9). Although "Inside the walls / world changes are planned, bosses overthrown," these people have little impact on the world outside the walls (10). Not feeling at home in the apartment, the narrator says, "the stars are the key / turning in the lock of night. / Turn the deadbolt and I am home. / I have walked to the dark earth, / opened a door to nights where there are no apartments, / just drumming and singing" (10). Traveling through her memory to the songs of an aunt, brothers, trees, and deer restores to her a feeling of meaning and belonging to the earth.

While living in Minneapolis, Hogan felt that her writing had become more "head writing" than before, that her language was faster paced, like the city environment" (Coltelli 82). Even so, as in her earlier work, much of the poetry in *Savings* (1987) accentuates the natural image as metaphor. In "Geraniums," as LaVonne Ruoff notes, "the flowers remain as a symbol of the life that burns in everything," including "red flowers / abandoned in an empty house" (17). This poem is about the urge to bloom, the plant like the human "exploding, wanting out, / wanting love / water / wanting" (17). Increasingly, Hogan probes the inner life, to find its heart.

The ever-changing, transforming life of the world is integral to such poems as "Breaking," which acknowledges that "we live / off those before us," not just our own parents, who raised us but those "that were here before our tribes, / that were here before the Americans / from broken worlds" (43). She develops this theme in *The Book of Medicines* (1993), using images that highlight primal elements of nature.

Life emerged from water. Images of creation out of the sea predominate in *The Book of Medicines*, which begins with "The History of Red." This account of creation begins in darkness, "some other order of things / never spoken" (9). Then new forms of life emerge from "black earth, / lake, the face of light on water" (9). The images of "human clay," "blood," "caves with red bison / painted in their own blood," "a new child / wearing the red, wet mask of birth," "this yielding land," "fear," "wounds," "red shadows of leeches," "fire" mirror the history of life on earth and chronicle the human suffering and strength that are necessary to survival.

The second part, "Hunger," explores the basic human need to satisfy the appetites for food and sex. Implicit is the notion that one cannot protect oneself from one's own greed or that of others unless one is willing to understand it. "Hunger crosses oceans" in the poem "Hunger," as fishermen hear the "songs of whales so large / the men grew small" (17). Hungry for sex and for power over women, the men "sat on the ship and cried" (17); "destitute," they "took the shining dolphins from the sea. / They were like women, / they said, / and had their way / with them" (18). "Hunger" is about understanding the need and also the greed that have led to the destruction of animals like the dolphin, the bear, and the buffalo and about the loneliness inherent in such a pursuit. In "Bear," Hogan says "we are safe / from the bear / and we have each other, / we have each other / to fear" (25).

In the third part, "The Book of Medicines," Hogan returns to beginnings to find the original power that can still be present in this world. Hogan's poetic vision spirals in this book, building on themes from her earlier work. In "Flood," the rain causes her to dream of "red turtles" and of "dark turtles, old and silent / with yellow, open eyes" (86). Though there are many animals in this section of the book, it is the human relationship to them, to other humans, and to the earth that she emphasizes.

These poems, with their many references to Chickasaw history and tradition, view breaking or tearing as essential in the process of creation and renewal. "Tear" is an account of the Trail of Tears of her ancestors, especially the women, who were forced to tear cloth to make dresses, since the soldiers had disarmed them of their scissors and knives. Revealing the power in "tear" and "live," with their dual meanings, Hogan ends this poem, "All around me are my ancestors, / my unborn children. / I am the tear between them / and both sides live" (60). Hogan has created a powerful ambiguity with her use of the homonyms *tear* and *tear*. Both meanings signify throughout this poem; thus the act of tearing the people from their land and of even forcing them to engage in the act of tearing is imbued with the emotion, the tears, that result from being torn.

The theme of severed relationships reaches a cosmic plane in the poem "Partings": "torn from her far beginnings / the moon was once earth, / a daughter whose leaving broke land to pieces" (71). This poem again illustrates Hogan's development of the mother–daughter theme, demonstrating the pain of separation, but also the new life that separation engenders.

There are strong poems about love between a man and a woman in this book. "Two" begins, "The weight of a man on a woman / is like falling into the river without drowning"(75); and "Nothing" ends, "it is the emptiness we love, touch, enter in one another / and try to fill" (76). In the final poem, "The Origins of Corn," planting corn is seen as "putting your love in the ground"(87). In this poem, Hogan brings together the seed, the sexual energy, the "medicines, / the corn song, / the hot barefoot dance"—essentials for assuring that "all things will grow / and the plants who climb into this world / will find it green and alive" (87). Her poems accentuate the power of words as energy to sustain the heartbeat of the earth.

Nesting in the Ruins:

The Poetry
of
Wendy Rose

Chapter

8

Giving voice to indigenous people, to women and children, Wendy Rose documents the historical and contemporary atrocities of American society. Speaking for human beings—rejected, used, sold, or worse—in a society that values the dollar above everything, even above the capacity for regeneration, Rose crafts poetry that is an uncompromising indictment of callous capitalism.

Rose first gained attention in the mid-seventies, when her poems and watercolor illustrations appeared in *Carriers of the Dream Wheel*. Rose's drawings extend the meaning of her poetry, adding another dimension to her words. By the end of the twentieth century, Rose had published nine books of poetry, and her poems were included in the major anthologies of Native American literature.

Born in Oakland, California, on May 7, 1948, Rose, whose original name was Bronwen Elizabeth Edwards, grew up in the Bay area, near Richmond. She has referred to herself as "physically separated from one-half of my family and rejected by the half that brought me up" (Bruchac, *Survival* 254). The ancestry of her mother, Betty Edwards, was Bear Valley Miwok, English, German, Scottish, and Irish (Swann and Krupat 256–57). Although there is some uncertainty as to the identity of her father, Rose believes he was Charles Loloma, a famous Hopi artist. However, she was raised by her mother and by Dick Edwards, a musician whose ancestry was Welsh, Scottish, and mixed Native American (from the Chico or Durham Rancheria and Missouri). Edwards, she has written, "seemed to hate" her. Rose suffered an unhappy childhood, which she has tried to exorcise in her art (Wendy Rose to Norma Wilson, October 4, 1999). In an autobiographical essay, she wrote, "As a child, I would run away from the beatings, from the obscene words, and always know that if I could run far enough, then any leaf, any insect, any bird, any breeze could bring me to my true home" (Swann and Krupat 255).

Raised a Roman Catholic, Rose began to explore her spirituality and cultural identity during her teenage years. She cofounded the Light of Dawn Temple, a group that studied metaphysical literature, and she began to seek her indigenous roots. In 1969, she joined in the occupation of Alcatraz Island, an assertion of Native American treaty rights.

During the 1970s she attended Cabrillo College, Contra Costa College, and the University of California, Berkeley, where she earned a B.A. (1976) and an M.A. (1978) and was a Ph.D. candidate in anthropology. As a student, Rose took few courses in writing and literature; however as a junior at Berkeley, she was enrolled in a poetry writing workshop with Josephine Miles. From 1979 to 1983 Rose taught in the Native American Studies Program at the University of California, Berkeley. She worked at the Lowie Museum of Anthropology at Berkeley and was editor of the *American Indian Quarterly*. She was a lecturer in Native American studies at California State University, Fresno, from 1983 to 1984. Thereafter she was the coordinator of American Indian studies at Fresno City College.

The search for identity that is central to Rose's art has extended from her own personal search to an empathy with others whose identities have been exploited for others' profits. As Andrew Wiget has pointed out, "Of all native poets now writing, none, with the possible exception of Momaday, has more consistently reasserted the creation of personal identity through art" (103).

The assertion of her Hopi identity is at the heart of Rose's first book, *Hopi Roadrunner Dancing* (1973), which she published under the self-given name Chiron Khanshendel. One of the poems, "Newborn Woman, May 7, 1948," is about having been unwanted by her parents. The refrain "i could not help it" is repeated throughout this poem. But the poem ends in self-affirmation:

> Dreams of my mother i shattered, i arrived. . . . i indian
> i desert, i newborn woman. (9)

Essential to Rose in this search was making contact with her father. In a tender poem, "Oh Father," she wrote of the closeness she felt to him: "fingertips melting into each other, / spirits merging" . . ."all I have to do is look into your eyes." The poem ends: "i'm sorry i guess / but i have to know: / oh father, who am I?" (11).

In 1977 Rose and her husband, Arthur Murata, traveled to Arizona to visit Charles Loloma, with whom her mother had had an affair, and who Rose believed was her father (Wendy Rose to Norma Wilson, October 4, 1999). She wrote of this visit in *Builder Kachina: A Home-Going Cycle* (1979). More grounded in and celebratory of place than her other books, *Builder Kachina* is about going back to find herself. This journey was essential to Rose as an artist and as a person: "Must I explain why / the songs are stiff and shy? / . . . / California moves my pen / but Hotevilla [pueblo] dashes through my blood / like a great / and crazy dragonfly" (n.p.).

Her poetry indicates that from Loloma she learned that building roots is a process: "Carefully / the way we plant the corn / in single places, each place / a hole just one finger around. / We'll build your roots / that way. . . . / . . . / What we can't find / we'll build but / slowly, / slowly" ("Builder Kachina"). This poem reveals the careful effort of a woman, whose community is urban Indian and pantribal, to understand her relationship to the land and her Native culture.

The Hopi people are linked by their language to the Aztecs and their Nahuatl descendants in the Valley of Mexico. Humans have inhabited the Western Pueblo region for more than twelve thousand years. When the Spanish first invaded their territory in 1540, there were numerous Hopi villages.

Like the other pueblo peoples, the Hopi suffered extreme cruelty at the hands of the Spanish. Hopi were severely punished for practicing their traditional religion. Spanish priests filled kivas, like the one at Awatovi, with sand and forced the Hopi to build Catholic churches on top of them (Rushforth et al. 101).

Immediately following the Pueblo Revolt of 1680, hundreds and perhaps thousands of Native people of the Rio Grande region left their homes and moved to the Hopi mesas. Some of these refugees built their own villages. Others were probably absorbed into Hopi society.

After the Spanish reconquest of the region, which occurred between 1692 and 1698, the Hopi pueblos, except for Awatovi, defied Spanish and Catholic domination. Early in the eighteenth century, Hopi from other villages destroyed much of Awatovi. When a terrible three-year drought came in 1777, Hopi villagers scattered into surrounding hills seeking wild food. Tenaciously they maintained their way of life. They resisted the Dawes Act of 1887, which sought to divide their land into allotments. Hotevilla, the home of Loloma, was established in 1906 by "hostile" refugees from Oraibi. Among the most conservative Hopi, residents of Hotevilla bitterly fought the extension of electrical utilities to their village in 1968. Though she did not herself grow up in the Hopi culture, Rose no doubt was influenced as a poet by the long history of Hopi resistance.

Having affirmed her identity in *Builder Kachina*, Rose uses an angry, ironic and pan-Indian voice in *Academic Squaw* (1977), which forms part of her later book, *Lost Copper* (1980). The poems in *Academic Squaw* are a direct result of her study of anthropology. They condemn the pricing of Native American cultures. "Three Thousand Dollar Death Song" is an outcry against the pricing of bones, because "bones are alive. They're not dead remnants but rather they're alive" (Bruchac, *Survival* 262). Treating Native Americans of the past not as anthropological specimens but as people whose lives and struggles are to be respected, *Academic Squaw* gives them voices and allows them to speak their pain. Combining her insights as a Native American with facts she learned in anthropological studies, and using a modernized dramatic-monologue poetic technique, Rose imagines the words of a Dakota woman killed in the Wounded Knee Massacre in "I Expected My Skin and My Blood to Ripen." As the poem opens, the woman voices her suffering:

I expected my skin and my blood
to ripen, not be ripped from my bones;
like fallen fruit I am peeled, tasted,
discarded; my seeds open and
have no future.. . . (n. p.)

But the woman's final words rise above her suffering as a statement of
power and spirituality:

Now
the ghost dances
impervious
to bullets.

That the brutal conquerors failed to recognize the power of the human
spirit to overcome the violence of colonization is one of Rose's messages in
these powerful poems.

Constantly moving back and forth between historical and contemporary contexts and between her own experiences and those of many other
people, Rose, like Simon Ortiz and Maurice Kenny, is a chronicler of the
larger American historical and social sphere. Yet, her travel books contain
more description and fewer historical and social critiques than her other
works. The poems in *What Happened When the Hopi Hit New York* (1982)
describe a journey across the United States, beginning in California and
proceeding to the Hopi Reservation, then across the United States to Brooklyn, with several stops along the way. The book ends with her flight back to
California. Her perceptive and often funny poems about the places she
visited describe the people who inhabit them. In "Punk Party Brooklyn
1978" she writes, "Like any party / they photograph each other but / forget
to develop / the film," taking note of the partygoers' focus on immediate
gratification and the shallow and ephemeral encounters she saw there (31).

What the Mohawk Made the Hopi Say (1993) is another travel book,
written in collaboration with Rose's friend Maurice Kenny. From Kenny,
Rose learned to appreciate the mountains of the Adirondacks, which she

had earlier considered merely hills: "I finally agree / turning into a rock / that these are mountains / noble as any / and all of Arizona / must wait / for spring thaw" (*Bone Dance* 69). Selections from *What Happened When the Hopi Hit New York* and *What the Mohawk Made the Hopi Say* are included along with parts of six other books in *Bone Dance: New and Selected Poems 1965–1993*.

In the same vein as *Academic Squaw*, Rose's book *The Halfbreed Chronicles* (1985) is perhaps her best. These poems are not pretty; they document the brutal ways that people have continued to exploit one another in what purports to be a civilized American culture. Combining her Native American sensibility and her knowledge as an anthropologist with the use of dramatic personae, a technique she used in *Academic Squaw*, Rose gives voice to Truganniny, Yuriko, and Julia, among others. These tortured women dramatize a few of the horrors of our time. In "Truganniny," the last Tasmanian utters her death wish: "put me where / they will not / find me" (57). The note that introduces this poem informs us that Truganniny, like her husband who died before her, was "stuffed, mounted and put on display for over eighty years."

In "Yuriko," a girl "born severely retarded" says of her mother, a victim of the bombing of Hiroshima: "Radiation / came like a man / and licked her thighs; / I was a tiny fish / boneless within / and I felt nothing" (64). Julia Pastrana, a Mexican Indian woman, was a mid-nineteenth-century singer and dancer in the circus, billed as "The Ugliest Woman in the World." After her death, her husband had her body and that of their infant son preserved and stuffed and charged circus audiences admission to see them. According to Rose's note, their bodies were exhibited as recently as 1975 in Europe and the U.S. In the poem "Julia," this woman, still wanting to believe that he loves her, appeals to her husband:

Tell me it was just a dream
my husband, a clever trick
made by some tin-faced village god
or ghost coyote, to frighten me
with his claim that our marriage is made
of malice and money. (69)

Whatever their suffering, Rose's personae are defiant. They rise from the ruins, in the manner of "Naawva Taawi," her modern Hopi fight song about the miraculous survival of the indigenous people, who have used the leavings of European culture to rebuild their own. This poem ends:

> See, Pahana
> how we nest
> in your ruins. (35)

Pahana, Rose explains in a footnote, means "whiteman" in the Hopi language and refers to a "way of life, a set of institutions, rather than to male human beings of European ancestry." She states the belief that "all of us, including such men, are victims of the 'whiteman.'"

Going to War With All My Relations (1993), later published in *Bone Dance*, is a direct consideration of Rose's family history as part of the larger panorama of American history. The title of one of the poems is "Margaret Newmann," the name of Rose's great-great-grandmother, born in Darmstadt, Germany, in 1832; she died in San Francisco in 1925. Rose says she traveled to "where the very streets were gold, gold on which / stolen kisses fall not gently at all and the / gun glimmers / from a thousand Spanish swords, ankle-deep / already / in Miwok bones" (*Bone Dance* 77). This ancestor, part of the "brave heritage / of Gold Rush California" (77), was also the source of the poet's "tongue made indigenous / by all the men you would love" (79). The poem accentuates the tribal origins of all peoples, including those who came to the Americas from Europe.

Yet most have distanced themselves from these natural origins. In "Mount Rushmore," Rose notes that "the whiteman has chiseled / the faces of his dead / on the very bones / of the hill" (*Bone Dance* 81). The whiteman has lost contact with the natural world and, as a result, "The very mountain / withholds its blessing. / Lizards scramble / to re-make its face" (81).

In "Excavation at Santa Barbara Mission" Rose begins with this statement in italics: "*When archaeologists excavated Santa Barbara Mission in California, they discovered human bones in the adobe walls.*" The poem is written from the point of view of an archaeologist who initially considers himself an artist with "pointed trowel" (*Bone Dance* 85). Gradually, as he digs and uncovers fragile bones, he comes to conceive of himself as a "hungry scientist / sustaining myself / with bones of / men and women asleep in the wall" (85). Like "communion wafers," the bones transform the archaeologist's consciousness. The final stanza repeats four times: "They built the mission with dead Indians" (85), emphasizing that this is an actual fact of history, not just a metaphor.

"Notes on a Conspiracy," like her earlier poems narrated by Native personae whose remains have been placed on exhibit, is an indictment of archaeologists who have no respect or understanding for the ancient peoples. Such "skullmongers" are "drowned in the blood of dead nations," suffocating in their "poisonous air" (*Bone Dance* 87).

To Rose, the imperialist's disrespect for people is not limited to Native American or ancient peoples. It is operative in her "Yellow Ribbons" poem, about the Gulf War. This poem, written in 1991, considers the real meaning of the yellow ribbon, then a national symbol representing America's desire for her soldiers' safe return. Rose's poem ends showing "strong young men / the future of a nation / dancing death postures / as they burn in their tanks, / . . . ragged white flags, / blasted to bits, truth retreating as Sand Creek's ghosts / sit on the memory of black bayonets" and "the blood-spattered parade, / around bewildered mothers, lost and weeping elders, / lonely voices that cry and beg for peace" (*Bone Dance* 89). Rose will not allow the yellow ribbons to hide the "yankee fist" of violence. Her poems, echoing condemnations of war that were uttered a century earlier by authors such as Mark Twain, enrage our social conscience.

The title of her book *Now Poof She Is Gone* (1994) is from the poem "Is It Crazy to Want to Unravel," which, like many of the poems in this book, is consciously expressive of a female consciousness. Like Meridel Le Sueur in *Rites of Ancient Ripening*, Rose identifies with the seeds of wildflowers and with the generations of "disobedient women" (95) who lived before her. Although the images in the poem are of women dissolving, evaporating, and disappearing, they are shown to have tremendous, invisible power: "I could fly apart / and watch my whirling blood / form galaxies in the air, / spatter on the men / who hammer to death / the trees and remark / that a woman just /

was standing there / and now / poof she is gone" (95). Nevertheless, that power is unseen by men whose vision can't penetrate surface appearances. Like Le Sueur, Rose writes from an uncompromisingly feminist vision that fiercely loves the earth and its people and speaks passionately for them.

Rose's poetry is personal, genealogical, and at the same time global. Rose believes that as a "halfbreed" who has survived, she has something important to do. Perhaps that something is to continue writing poems that cause us to reexamine and end our mistreatment of those who do not easily fit into any one narrow category of human beings.

The Ground Speaks:

The Poetry of
Joy
Harjo

Chapter

9

In Joy Harjo's poetry, the ground speaks through voices of people intimately related to the earth. Believing that "the word *poet* is synonymous with truth-teller," Harjo uses a voice that is passionate and strong, ringing with anger and joy, love and pain, and always longing for the spirit's dance. Seeking a state of balance, honoring those who are true to their vision, her voice is constantly evolving toward an increasingly diverse and complex expression of the history of this land.

Born in Tulsa, Oklahoma, on May 9, 1951, to Allen W. and Wynema Baker Foster, Harjo is Cherokee on her mother's side and Muscogee (Creek) on her father's. The Muscogee traditionally named people *Harjo* (or *Hadjo*) for their courage. The family included a long line of tribal leaders and orators, including Monahwee, who led the Red Stick War against Andrew Jackson's army. An enrolled member of the Muscogee Tribe, Harjo credits her great aunt, Lois Harjo Ball (1906–82), to whom she dedicated her book *She Had Some Horses* (1983), with having taught her much of her Indian identity. Her great-aunt and her grandmother, both of whom completed bachelor's degrees in fine arts in the early 1900s, inspired her artistic development.

Harjo grew up in north Tulsa among mixed-blood families. Her neighbors were of white, Seminole, Pawnee, and other identities. Partly because alcohol was a problem in Joy's childhood home, she left Oklahoma to attend high school at the Institute of American Indian Arts in Santa Fe. There she developed as a graphic artist, graduating in 1968. That same year she gave birth to a son in Tahlequah, Oklahoma, an experience she recalls in her essay "Warrior Road," from *Reinventing the Enemy's Language* (Harjo and Bird). In 1970, Joy Foster, with her family's permission, took the surname of her paternal grandmother, Naomi Harjo. Rainy Dawn, her daughter, was born in 1972 in Albuquerque when Harjo was an art student at the University of New Mexico. During the interval between her children's births, Harjo worked as a waitress, a service station attendant, and a nursing assistant; she also cleaned hospital rooms and led a health spa dance class.

Harjo completed a B.A. in English at the University of New Mexico in 1976. She then studied at the Writer's Workshop at the University of Iowa, completing an M.F.A. in creative writing in 1978. Harjo studied filmmaking at the Anthropology Film Center, Santa Fe, in 1982.

She has served as contributing editor of *Contact II* and poetry editor of *High Plains Literary Review* and on the boards of directors of the National Association for Third World Writers and the Native American Public Broadcasting Consortium. She has been on the policy panel for the National Endowment for the Arts.

Harjo has taught at the Institute of American Indian Arts, Arizona State University, the University of Montana, the University of Colorado, the University of Arizona, the University of New Mexico, and the University of California. Her poetry is included in most major anthologies of Native American poetry as well as a number of anthologies of American literature. In October 2000 Harjo received a Lifetime Achievement Award from the Western Literature Association.

Harjo began writing poetry at the age of twenty-two after hearing a reading by Simon Ortiz at the University of New Mexico. Other literary influences are Leslie Marmon Silko, Flannery O'Connor, James Wright, Pablo Neruda, Meridel Le Sueur, Galway Kinnell, Leo Romero, Audre Lorde, Louis Oliver, and June Jordan.

As John Scarry pointed out in his essay "Representing Real Worlds: The Evolving Poetry of Joy Harjo"(1992), her experiences as an artist, a filmmaker, and a musician have all influenced her poetry (286). Harjo told Marilyn Kallet in an interview published in the *Kenyon Review* (1993), "I made the decision to work with words and the power of words, to work with language, yet I approach the art as a visual artist" (57).

Harjo's poetry conveys her connections to the places where she and her ancestors have lived—northeastern Oklahoma, the Southwest, the southeastern United States, and Hawaii. The poetry in Harjo's first book, *The Last Song*, published in 1975, voices her strong connection to the landscape, history, and Native people of Oklahoma and the Southwest. Images in the title poem of that collection indicate her understanding that her breath had evolved from "an ancient chant" that her "mother knew" (*What Moon Drove Me to This?* 67). Acknowledging that the land she had left behind was still part of her body and voice, she wrote, "oklahoma will be the last song / i'll ever sing." In a "Bio-Poetics Sketch" for *Greenfield Review* (1981) Harjo recalls that digging in the "dark rich earth" as a child was a formative experience in her development as a poet. Like three other southeastern indigenous cultures, Harjo's Muscogee and Cherokee ancestors were forcibly moved to Indian Territory, now Oklahoma, in the late 1830s. They carried with them their memories of life in Georgia, Tennessee, Mississippi, and Alabama. Ancestral memories conveyed to Harjo by her relatives live in her poetry.

Some of her early poems indicate Harjo's feeling of relatedness to Native Americans of other tribes. In "3 AM," for example, she writes of "trying to find a way back" to "a part of the center / of the world," or Old Oraibi, a Hopi village on Arizona's Third Mesa (*What Moon Drove Me to This?* 43). This village is perhaps the oldest indigenous community in North America.

Other early poems focus on the lives of Native women. "Conversations Between Here and Home" expresses a strong concern and respect for women who have suffered abuse by men and who are struggling to rebuild their lives: "angry women are building / houses of stones / they are grinding the mortar / between straw-thin teeth / and broken families" (*What Moon Drove Me to This?* 18). Like Linda Hogan, Harjo emphasizes women's capacity to be self-reliant and to provide for their children's needs.

Besides focusing on the land, Native cultural history, and the lives of women, some of Harjo's early poetry expresses frustration with communication in contemporary America, as people increasingly attempt to communicate by telephone and electronic mail rather than face to face. In "Are You Still There" the narrator finds it difficult to talk to the man she has called. His voice overwhelms her as he says, "'i have missed you'" and the narrator's voice "caught / shredded on a barbed wire fence / . . . / flutters soundless in the wind" (*What Moon Drove Me to This?* 52). The distance between the two seems characteristic of the modern, technological world in which Native people are separated from the land and from one another, largely as a result of Europeans' having taken the land from them; it was Europeans who put up barbed wire to keep their cattle in and to establish their claims to the land.

These poems from Harjo's first book are included in her second book, *What Moon Drove Me to This?* (1979), whose publication led to attention and acclaim from literary critics such as Andrew Wiget and Paula Gunn Allen. Wiget says, "At her best the energy generated by this journeying creates a powerful sense of identity that incorporates everything into the poetic self, so that finally she can speak for all the earth" (*Native American Literature* 117). Noting that Harjo's poetry combines "ancient understandings of the moon, of relationship, of womanhood, and of journeying with city streets, rodeo grounds, highways, airports, Indian bars, and powwows," Allen says, "From the meeting of the archaic and the contemporary the facts of her life become articulate." (160). Allen calls Harjo "a poet whose work is concerned with metaphysical as well as social connections" (*Sacred Hoop* 166). A woman in "White Sands" realizes that unlike her sister, who will wear a wedding gown, she does not fit her mother's ideal image. But the woman's image of herself—"I will be dressed in / the clear blue sky"(9)— gives her, as Allen has stated, an "unbroken and radiant connection with something larger and more important than a single individual," her mother, a connection to the cosmos itself (*Sacred Hoop* 124). Harjo's poetry evolves from her own personal experience, but her vision consistently moves outward.

Harjo's third book, *She Had Some Horses,* develops many of her earlier poetic themes. "For Alva Benson and for Those Who Have Learned to Speak" again considers the experience of Native women and their relationship to the land: "And the ground spoke when she was born. / Her mother heard it. In Navajo she answered / as she squatted down against the earth / to give birth" (*She Had Some Horses* 18). Women like Alva Benson, who remain grounded, knowing the land as their source of life and consciously affirming their relationship to it, are symbols of strength and continuity in Harjo's poetry. However, rather than romanticizing the lives of

Native American women, Harjo writes truthfully about the fragmented families of many of them and their consequent suffering.

Some women in Harjo's poems long for the security of a family and a home that many people living in cities have lost. Her powerfully moving poem "The Woman Hanging from the Thirteenth Floor Window" describes a woman "hanging by her own fingers, her / own skin, her own thread of indecision / . . . / . . . crying for / the lost beauty of her own life" (*She Had Some Horses* 23). The woman hanging becomes a metaphor for "all the women of the apartment / building who stand watching her, stand watching themselves" (23).

Harjo's visit to the Chicago Indian Center planted the seed for the poem. The image of the woman hanging, though imagined, seems so real that women have often approached Harjo to tell her they have known the woman in the poem or have read a newspaper article about her ("The Woman Hanging" 40).

The woman hanging is in many ways similar to the character Noni Daylight, referred to by Patricia Clark Smith as a "kind of alter ego" in Harjo's poems. In "Kansas City," "Noni Daylight's / a dishrag wrung out over bones" (*She Had Some Horses* 33). Could there be a more precise metaphor for a worn-out woman? Yet this woman accepts her life, choosing "to stay / in Kansas City, raise the children / she had by different men, / all colors. Because she knew / that each star rang with separate / colored hue, as bands of horses / and wild / like the spirit in her" (33).

Harjo's use of repetition in *She Had Some Horses* creates a chantlike impression, as in this excerpt from "The Woman Hanging from the Thirteenth Floor Window": "She thinks of Carlos, of Margaret, of Jimmy. / She thinks of her father, and of her mother. / She thinks of all the women she has been, of all / the men. She thinks of the color of her skin, and / of Chicago streets, and of waterfalls and pines. / She thinks of moonlight nights, and of cool spring storms" (23). Here Harjo's use of anaphora, balanced phrasing, inclusive language, and the woman's appreciation of the natural world echo the style of traditional oral songs. Such characteristics are consistent with Harjo's belief in the power of language. Harjo is convinced that, as in ceremonies, stories, and oratory, the use of repetition in poems can transform a statement into a "litany," giving the participant or reader "a way to enter in to what is being said and a way to emerge whole but changed"

("The Woman Hanging" 39). It is the repetition not only of words but also of sounds and rhythms that energizes Harjo's poetry. C. B. Clark has observed, "A cadence marks her work that is reminiscent of the repetitions of the Indian ceremonial drum" (3117). Harjo's cadence is one of the poetic elements she uses to empower the people who read her poems.

In *She Had Some Horses*, as in Harjo's earlier poetry, nonhuman elements are understood as integral and related to the human body. The strong, chantlike rhythm of the title poem emphasizes the parallel between human psychological states and various kinds of horses, remythologizing the horse in contemporary culture. The horses represent diverse facets of an individual's psyche, or various types of people, from the aloof and self-centered to the servant of others. The horses also represent various elements of nature, from "bodies of sand" to "blue air of sky" (63–64). Moving toward an acceptance of the whole human condition, Harjo blends human and nonhuman nature and conflicting feelings and attitudes, acknowledging the constant duality of love and hate between human beings who are emotionally close to one another.

Alcoholism and its emotional distancing is her topic in "Night Out." As they try "another shot, anything to celebrate this deadly / thing called living," Indians find themselves trapped: "You have paid the cover charge thousands of times over / with your lives / and now you are afraid / you can never get out" (21). Alcoholism, as Harjo's poetry illustrates, not only traps adults in the bars but is passed on to youth as well. "The Friday before the Long Weekend" expresses frustration with trying to teach a "drunk child." Still, Harjo expresses the hope that someday the alcoholic child will come to an awareness such as that of the woman in her poem "Alive," who learns to accept herself as a part of creation.

Through imagery that is often surreal, Harjo's poetry exposes the United States history of colonization and oppression of Native Americans and people of color, a pattern that continues in the modern era. Her surrealistic poem "Backwards" speaks of the colonizers' wasteful destruction: "The moon came up white, and torn / at the edges. I dreamed I was / four that I was standing on it. / A whiteman with a knife cut pieces / away / and threw the meat / to the dogs" (*She Had Some Horses* 20).

John Scarry has praised the "poetic fluidity of Harjo's simultaneous physicality and spirituality, and her ability to combine the eternal past and the continuing present" (287). "New Orleans," which addresses the colonization of Creek culture, exemplifies her poetry's simultaneity and timelessness. The poem describes the Spanish conquistador De Soto as "one of the ones who yearned / for something his heart wasn't big enough / to handle. / (And DeSoto thought it was gold)" (*She Had Some Horses* 43). But the Creeks "lived in earth towns, / not gold, / spun children, not gold" (43). According to the poem, the Creeks drowned De Soto in the Mississippi. Nevertheless, Harjo says, "I know I have seen DeSoto, / having a drink on Bourbon Street / mad and crazy / dancing with a woman as gold / as the river bottom" (44). Harjo's poem releases buried Creek voices to tell the story of their powerful generative life and of their destruction. Her description of De Soto dancing with a Creole woman presents an image of reverse assimilation, a historical reality in which the influence of the land and Native culture has been pervasive although unacknowledged. Everywhere the cities, rivers, all the places on the American land speak of their history, but only to those who are patient enough to listen.

She Had Some Horses is an exorcism of the kind of fear that can paralyze an individual or a culture. Harjo confronts oppressors past and present in her chantlike poem "I Give You Back": from the individual perspective—"I am not afraid to be hungry. / I am not afraid to be full. / I am not afraid to be hated. / I am not afraid to be loved. / to be loved, to be loved, fear" (73–74) and from the cultural perspective—"I give you back to the white soldiers / who burned my home, beheaded my children, / raped and sodomized my brothers and sisters. / I give you back to those who stole the / food from our plates when we were starving" (73). Through a "fierce anger" and her courage to name the enemy and describe injustice and suffering, Harjo frees herself; and, through her litany of words, her readers. She makes her poetry a force for social change. Consistent with the traditional Native American respect for language, Harjo told Joseph Bruchac in an interview published in his book *Survival This Way* (1987), "I realize writing can help change the world. I'm aware of the power of language which isn't meaningless words. . . . Sound is an extension of all, and sound is spirit, motion" (100).

Overcoming fear of various forms of oppression is a central theme in

She Had Some Horses. But in her poem "Transformations," first published in *Harper's Anthology of 20th Century Native American Poetry* and later included in her fifth book, *In Mad Love and War* (1990), Harjo began to emphasize not just overcoming fear through resistance but healing one's psychological wounds through love. Calling transformation "the oldest tribal ceremonial theme," Paula Allen says that "it comes once again into use with the American Indian poetry of extinction and regeneration" (*Sacred Hoop* 162). Harjo calls her "Transformations" a "letter" addressed to someone who "would like to destroy" her (*In Mad Love and War* 59). Rejecting revenge, the poem continues, "Bone splintered in the eye of one you choose / to name your enemy won't make it better for you to see." Instead, the poem calls for a transformation from hatred to love.

The prose poems of *Secrets from the Center of the World* move from an inward to an outward vision, responding to the landscape photography of Stephen Strom. In her response to the wonderful desert scenes painted by Strom's camera eye, Harjo is ecstatic and philosophical: "I can hear the sizzle of newborn stars, and know that anything of meaning, of fierce magic is emerging here. I am witness to flexible eternity, the evolving past, and I know we will live forever, as dust or breath in the face of stars, in the shifting pattern of winds" (56). *Secrets* focuses on the healing quality of the earth and the vision of spirituality that are central to Harjo's poetry.

Nature as healer is also a focus of *In Mad Love and War*, which presents a mixture of cultures and of humanity and inhumanity. From "Deer Dancer," set in a dingy bar, to the blues lament "Strange Fruit," set in a rural area of the United States, to "Resurrection," set in Nicaragua, the poems in this collection tell the horrible truth about oppression while at the same time celebrating the beautiful natural world. Harjo was awarded numerous prizes for *In Mad Love and War*. It won the Poetry Society of America's William Carlos Williams Award, New York University's Delmore Schwartz Memorial Poetry Prize, and the PEN Oakland Josephine Miles Award.

Harjo's perspective on life at the end of the century forms a strong contrast to that of early-twentieth-century poets Yeats and Eliot. Comparing Harjo's accomplishment of setting, mood, and vision in her poem "Deer Dancer" to the visionary poetry of William Butler Yeats, John Scarry says that "'Deer Dancer' may be seen as something of a Native American 'Second Coming'" (290). He points out that the "sterility of the landscape and the objective yet involved tone of Harjo's speaker" are similar to the landscape and tone of Yeats's poem. Yet, he continues, "'Deer Dancer' more directly invites the reader to share in the humanity of the 'Indian ruins' sitting so desolately in our native land-scape"(290). Unlike Yeats, whose poem questions and fears the coming of the new century, and Eliot, who sees his landscape as a wasteland, Harjo's "Deer Dancer" presents the woman dancing in a dingy bar as a blessing and promise.

Southern culture, blues music, and anger were ripening agents for Harjo's poem "Strange Fruit," a dramatic monologue reminiscent of those written earlier by Wendy Rose. The title is borrowed from a blues song writ-ten by Lewis Allen and recorded by Billie Holiday in 1939. A graphic and metaphorical description of lynching and a lamentation for the "strange fruit hangin' from the poplar trees," the song was declared "unsuitable for transmission" by the British Broadcasting Corporation when first released, and American radio stations were "wary of playing it," but the song made Holiday famous (Maddocks 45).

Harjo's vision in "Strange Fruit" moves between historical and con-temporary contexts. This broad vision, far from contradicting the world view of Native Americans, is consistent with their philosophical understand-ing of reciprocity and the interrelatedness of the universe. In the poem, Harjo blends the history of lynchings of African American men with the 1986 lynching in California of NAACP organizer Jacqueline Peters. It is impossible to distinguish the voice of Harjo from that of Peters. Both enunci-ate the ravages of racism and bigotry. And maybe that is Harjo's point. She transcends her own culturally specific background to link the victimization of her own people to the oppression of others. Harjo tells the bitter truth, with a spiritual strength that affirms the worth of a woman killed by racial hatred.

"Strange Fruit" emphasizes how little has changed since the violent eras of slavery and Jim Crow. The poem is dedicated to Jacqueline Peters, who was hanged from an olive tree in Lafayette, California, in 1986. Peters had been working to organize a local NAACP chapter in response to the 1985 lynching of a twenty-three-year-old black man. Written from the voice of a woman being lynched, and incorporating blues language and rhythms, the poem ends:

I didn't do anything wrong. I did not steal from your mother. My brother did not take your wife. I did not break into your home, tell you how to live or die. Please. Go away, hooded ghosts from hell on earth. I only want heaven in my baby's arms, my baby's arms. Down the road through the trees I see the kitchen light on my lover fixing supper, the baby fussing for her milk, waiting for me to come home. The moon hangs from the sky like a swollen fruit.

My feet betray me, dance anyway from this killing tree. (11–12)

Like "Strange Fruit," many of the other poems of *In Mad Love and War* are prose poetry, stretching wide across the page, consistent with their broad scope. Whether it's the quincentennial story or yesterday's murder, the history of this ground is injustice and pain. But many of Harjo's poems transcend this earth, speaking beyond to the world of the spirit. They express what survival must ultimately be about, the perception of what Harjo calls the "amazed world" (8).

In "For Anna Mae Pictou Aquash, Whose Spirit is Present Here and in the Dappled Stars (for we remember the story and must tell it again so we may all live)," she addresses the spirit of a Micmac woman who died in February 1976 on the Pine Ridge Reservation in South Dakota. When her body was buried, Aquash had not been identified, and the coroner said she had died of exposure. After it was discovered that the body was that of American Indian Movement member Aquash, the investigation was reopened, the body was exhumed, and a second autopsy was performed. Many people were outraged to learn that, rather than taking fingerprints to identify her, the first coroner had cut off Aquash's hands and turned them over to an FBI agent. The second autopsy also revealed that Aquash had been killed by a bullet fired at the back of her head, at close range. Speaking to the ghost of Aquash in the poem, Harjo writes: "Anna Mae, / everything and nothing changes. / You are the shimmering young woman / who found her voice, / when you were warned to be silent, or have your body cut away / from you like an elegant weed. / You are the one whose spirit is present in the dappled stars" (7). The poem ends by relating Aquash to the ghost dancers and to the spirit world: "we have just begun to perceive the amazed world the ghost dancers / entered / crazily, beautifully" (8). Only at the end of the twentieth century, through the voices of Native American writers like Harjo, did literature begin to consider the Ghost Dance with a proper respect for the movement and the dancers.

Harjo's next book is entitled *The Woman Who Fell from the Sky* (1994), which is also folklorists' title for an Iroquois creation story in which a young woman in the sky vault becomes the bride of the sun. When she becomes pregnant, the sun suspects her of adultery. In anger, he uproots the tree of life in the sky and flings her down into the opening. As she falls, ducks flock under her to cushion her descent, and she is later assisted by other animals, who make it possible for her to have a home on the Earth.

Harjo's cycle of stories, which parallel this Iroquoian cosmology, describe the experience of Native Americans in the twentieth century. Her title poem is the narrative of Lila, who met Johnny when they were children at an Indian boarding school. Johnny left to join the army and went to Vietnam. After graduation Lila worked days cleaning houses and nights at Dairy Queen. During the time the two were apart, Johnny named himself "Saint Coincidence," and Lila gave birth to three children. Having leaped into the "forbidden place," Lila has fallen but is rescued in front of the Safeway by Johnny, or Saint Coincidence. Coming together seems to be their destiny. In a commentary that follows the prose poem, Harjo describes traveling "far above the earth for a different perspective" (10). Through this spiritual travel, she has "understood love to be the very gravity holding each leaf, each cell, this earthy star together" (10). Lila and Johnny may have fallen, but they are still capable of loving and reviving each other. The transformation theme is important throughout this book.

In "The Place the Musician Became a Bear," Harjo links her own interest in jazz to musician Jim Pepper and to their Creek ancestry: "I've always believed us Creeks . . . had something to do with the origins of jazz. After all, when the African peoples were forced here for slavery they were brought to the traditional lands of the Muscogee peoples" (52). Always open to her creative potential as an artist, Harjo taught herself to play saxophone when she was in her thirties, then sought out Muscogee and Kaw jazz saxophonist Jim Pepper, who encouraged her. Harjo plays soprano and alto saxophone and recites her poetry with Poetic Justice, an all-Native American band. Other members of the group are Susan Williams, John Williams, Frank Poocha, Richard Carbajal, and William Bluehorse Johnson. The idea for the band was conceived in 1992, when Susan Williams and Harjo got together in Williams's garage and wrote the first drafts of a tune together for Harjo's poem about Anna Mae Aquash. Their CD, *Letter from the End of the Twentieth Century,* features "For Anna Mae Pictou Aquash . . ." as well as nine other poems. In concert, Harjo's voice is powerful, clearly extending the long and continuing tradition of the revolutionary spirit.

The music of Poetic Justice accompanies Harjo's reading of ten of the poems in *The Woman Who Fell From the Sky* on a cassette sold with the book. The poem "Reconciliation" opens the book in an attitude of acceptance and love: "All acts of kindness are lights in the war for justice" (n.p.). Many poems in this collection link Muscogee myths to the stories of modern people, ideas, or happenings that inspired Harjo's myth making.

Harjo dedicates two poems to her granddaughters, Haleigh Sara Bush and Krista Rae Chico, whose births are associated with rain. "The Naming," for Haleigh, places her granddaughter within the context of her female ancestry and her environment. Out of "wind bringing rain" and lightning her granddaughter was born. Harjo writes, "My grandmother is the color of night as she tells me to move away from the window when it is storming. *The lightning will take you*" (11). But the poem ends, "The earth is wet with happiness" (12). In an autobiographical note following the poem, Harjo tells of her maternal grandmother, Leona May Baker, whom Harjo did not especially like when she was a child. But with the approaching birth of her own granddaughter, she decided to find out more about this grandmother. After hearing her mother's story about her grandmother, Harjo "began to have compassion for this woman who was weighted down with seven children and no opportunities" (13). And when her granddaughter, Haleigh, was born, Harjo "felt the spirit of this grandmother in the hospital room" and "welcomed her" (13).

Leona May Baker's life, like that of many others in this book, was marred by violence. Returning after working for nine months on the railroad, Harjo's grandfather had found her grandmother pregnant with another man's child. He beat her so severely that she "went into labor and gave birth to the murdered child." After that, the two "attempted double suicide. They stood on the tracks while a train bore down on them as all the children watched in horror" (13). The two escaped death when Harjo's grandfather pushed her grandmother off the tracks and leaped to safety just in time.

In this book, as in all her work, Harjo illustrates the larger meaning of everyday experience. The book ends at the kitchen table in the poem "Perhaps the World Ends Here": "The gifts of the earth are brought and prepared, set on the table. So it has been since creation, and it will go on" (68). Here, in the mundane center of the house, the cosmic meaning of living and eating is contained. Harjo and Gloria Bird also made "Perhaps the World Ends Here" the final poem in their anthology *Reinventing the Enemy's Language: Contemporary Native Women's Writings of North America* (1997). This book affirms the act of writing as a way of maintaining sanity and strength through a natural process of creation. Women from fifty indigenous nations celebrate birth giving and their elemental connections. Above all, they value their spirituality as a means of gaining the vision and strength to live in good ways. Alongside the work of established poets such as Leslie Silko, Linda Hogan, Louise Erdrich, Elizabeth Cook-Lynn, Paula Gunn Allen, Mary TallMountain, and Wendy Rose are poems by women little known or published for the first time. Though the book presents an expansive vision of the indigenous women across the Americas, the writing is so intimate, it could have been spoken by women gathered for a feast.

Harjo entered the new century with *A Map to the Next World: Poems and Tales* (2000). The final line of the title poem, "You must make your own map," suggests the necessity of knowing one's own history and identity in the spiritual journey of living (21). In the prose and poetry of this book, Harjo recalls her entire experience, spiraling backward from her life in Honolulu at the beginning of the twenty-first century, to consider the significance and larger realities of life on the planet. Harjo asserts that the world is held together with the passionate intensity of love, which is affirmed in the ancient stories of Hawaiians, in memories of Harjo's parents greeting the dawn, and in her own love stories: "We are closer to the gods than we ever thought possible" (13).

Harjo's poetry is a medicine and a prayer to heal the divisions within and between human beings on this planet. From myth to reality and back again, Joy Harjo continues to write of America's past, our present, and our future in poetry that affirms our life spirit, condemning injustice, lamenting suffering, and speaking for this earth.

The New Generation

The number of Native American poets has at least doubled since the late sixties, when their poems were first anthologized. Forty-three poets are included in John E. Smelcer and D. L. Birchfield's *Durable Breath* (1994). Alongside early poems by established authors such as Robert Conley and James Welch are new poems by their contemporaries: Jim Barnes, Joseph Bruchac, Barney Bush, Anita Endrezze, Diane Glancy, Joy Harjo, Linda Hogan, Maurice Kenny, Duane Niatum, Nila northSun, Simon Ortiz, Carter Revard, Wendy Rose, and Ralph Salisbury. Also included are works by younger poets Sherman Alexie, Jeannette Armstrong, D. L. Birchfield, Kimberly Blaeser, E. K. Caldwell, Annie Hansen, Tiffany Midge, Cheryl Savageau, and Elizabeth Woody. This anthology gives overdue attention to poets from the north country. Of these, the poems of Cheryl Savageau, an Abenaki and French-Canadian writer, are the most remarkable. Rooted in the tradition of her Abenaki poet predecessor Joseph Bruchac, Savageau in "To Human Skin" remembers her father, whose "heart was green and growing, / as if he'd lived for centuries / an old forest tree man / rooted in the rocky soil / now called new england" (132). "Trees" pays tribute to her father, who taught her, as she is teaching her children, to love the white birch, "to lean / their cheeks against / the powdery white and hear / the heartbeat of the tree" (131). Savageau's poetry in her book *Dirt Road Home* (1995) is open hearted and direct in its portrayals of the mixed-blood people with whom she was raised.

Editors Larry Evers and Ofelia Zepeda celebrated twenty-five years of their journal *Sun Tracks* in a volume entitled *Home Places* (1995). Reflecting the purpose of this journal, "to suggest the continuum of imaginative verbal expression that is produced and enjoyed in Native American communities at the end of the twentieth century" (viii), the volume includes poems by well-established writers such as Ortiz, Henson, Hogan, Rose, Momaday, and Revard, alongside bilingual poets such as George Blueeyes, Daniel Lopez, Felipe S. Molina, and Ralph Cameron, who write first in their indigenous languages. Also included are poems by Elizabeth Woody, speaking from the perspective of a new generation with roots in the ancient life of her culture.

"In Memory of Crossing the Columbia" is about her mixed Native origins:

My board and blanket were Navajo
but my bed is inside the River.
In the beads of remembrance,
I am her body in my father's hands. (45)

Born in 1959 in Ganado, Arizona, of Navajo and Warm Springs Wasco ancestry, Woody is a member of the Confederated Tribes of Warm Springs, Oregon. Life in both the Southwest and the Northwest and the indigenous cultures of both parents and both landscapes have influenced her poetry. Her first collection, *Hand into Stone,* won an American Book Award in 1990. These poems were reprinted in Woody's *Seven Hands, Seven Hearts: Prose and Poetry.* Also a visual artist, Woody illustrated Sherman Alexie's book *Old Shirts & New Skins* (1993).

In 1994 *Sun Tracks* published Woody's *Luminaries of the Humble.* Her preface states that these poems grew out of her studies with poet Gail Trembley after Ofelia Zepeda asked her to submit a book manuscript at the 1992 Returning the Gift Festival of Native writers in Oklahoma. Woody's poems are thematically and stylistically similar to the poetry of Meskwaki poet Ray Young Bear. Paralleling his poem's title, "The Invisible Musician," Woody's "The Invisible Dress" bears something of the same message as

Young Bear—The material object or being that can be perceived through the senses carries with it a long tradition and history. One learns respect from such a poem: "Infinite in this dress, together, / brought back through hardship and inexplicable turmoil, / we emerge, again, wearing this dress, necessary / and radiantly fearless" (105). In Young Bear's title poem, "The Invisible Musician" is the frog. In her preface to *Luminaries*, Woody says that she also wants "to give voice to those who are not often heard from, like the salmon, forest trees, our little relatives that nourish us, the edible roots, berries, deer. All that may die from our neglect" (xiv). Like Young Bear, Woody utilizes a high level of abstract diction in her poetry. In "Translation of Blood Quantum," she writes, "We are watched over / by the mountains, not Man, not Monarchy, / or any other manifestations / of intimidation by misguided delusion of supremacy / over the Land or beings animate or inanimate" (103). And here, like Young Bear, she writes insightfully of human insignificance.

Woody's poem "Straight and Clear" asserts that the Native people are indicators for the rest of humankind that pollution of the environment is threatening our survival as a species: "indicator species are passed off as obstacles / to change in resource management. Evidence is tangible / as the bold print of cancer collects in the down winders / of the Hanford Nuclear Reservation. The difficult colloquies / of a people who are marked as expendables" (114).

First, as she says in "The Luminaries of the Humble," Native people are made poor by the taking of their land, "hauled out piece by piece, as lumber, salmon, and fruit"; then they are made sick by the radioactive contamination of their environment. The nuclear industry continuously looks to Native lands as locations for mining, power production, or waste facilities.

Like their predecessors, the new Native poets are committed to the land. Anishinabe environmentalist Winona LaDuke says, "The native struggle in North America today can only be properly understood as a pursuit of the recovery of land rights which are guaranteed through treaties" (Churchill 4). Their poetry tends to focus on contemporary experience on the land, yet the poetry of the new generation of Native writers also displays an awareness of the entire history of the land and its inhabitants. Sherman Alexie, one of the most prominent and prolific Native poets, is no exception. Alexie grew up in the Northwest, close to his Native roots. A registered member of the Spokane Nation, he attended school on the Spokane Reservation in Wellpinit, Washington, until he transferred to the high school in Reardan. He studied at Gonzaga University from 1985 to 1987 and at Washington State University from 1988 to 1991. Alex Kuo's creative writing class at W.S.U. got Alexie's ballpoint rolling. Alexie is probably most famous for his screenplay *Smoke Signals* (1998), which was the first widely distributed feature film that had been written, directed, and coproduced by Native Americans. In his introduction to the screenplay, Alexie says his love of movies is even greater than his love of books and that "screenplays are more like poetry than fiction" (*Smoke Signals* x); he compares their form to that of sonnets, but his question, "who is writing the free verse screenplays?," suggests that Alexie may think of his script as free-verse poetry.

Alexie made a grand entrance on the literary scene in 1992 with a chapbook of poems, *I Would Steal Horses,* and a book, *The Business of Fancydancing: Stories and Poems.* These were followed by a book of poems, *Old Shirts & New Skins,* and then in 1993 by *First Indian on the Moon,* a collection of short prose pieces and poetry. Though appreciated primarily for his sense of humor and his realistic juxtaposition of pop culture with Native life, the natural environment of the Spokane people is always in Alexie's consciousness. As Susan Brill has pointed out, Alexie's early books present a somewhat bleak view of reservation life. Yet, one sees a rising sense of optimism in *First Indian on the Moon* (1993). This more hopeful outlook springs in part from Alexie's increasing emphasis on his people's relationship with their environment.

Alexie addresses this relationship in his early poem "Grandmother." She is described as an "old crow of a woman in bonnet, sifting through the dump /salvaging those parts of the world / neither useless nor usefull" (*The Business of Fancydancing* 23). Juxtaposed with and following these lines is the next striking stanza: "she would be hours in the sweatlodge / come out naked and brilliant in the sun / steam rising off her body in winter / like a slow explosion of horses" (23). The purification ceremony is a means of rebirth, and horses are harbingers of hope throughout Alexie's poetry and prose. Both the dump and the sweatlodge are familiar places to Grandmother, who, like all of us, is surrounded every day by both the mundane and the spiritual. The relationship of Grandmother to the land is transmitted to a younger generation of women through her loving touch: "she braided my sister's hair that smelled deep / roots buried in the earth" (23).

Alexie's view of women is definitely more positive than his view of men. He wrote in "Spokane Tribal Celebration, September 1987" from *The Business of Fancydancing:* "I / know the only time Indian men / get close to the earth anymore is when Indian men / pass out and hit the ground" (74). Yet one can see in his later works an effort to understand what has made some Native American men become addicted to alcohol. By *First Indian On the Moon* (1993), Alexie was able to write in his poem "The Native American Broadcasting System": "do as the great Indian chiefs of the past / and leave everything / the way you found it but nobody loves a drunken Indian / anger in his heart, bitter / and more than a little confused" (86). The modern Indian man, Alexie's poem suggests, suffers from a fragmented life in which he has been given "a manual / for home improvement / without a table of contents" and "keys / to a door, a door that don't belong to no house" (87).

In his poem "Split Decisions" Alexie affirms Muhammad Ali's courage and poetics: "Mohammed Ali's poetry floated like a butterfly and stung like a bee. *We should all write exactly that way*" (90). The poem praises Ali for standing up to Uncle Sam and saying, *"I won't fight in Vietnam. I ain't got no quarrel with those Viet Cong"* (89), for refusing to tell anything but the truth. This is a classic twentieth-century poem, with a strong ending, "he stood up" (91). Like much of Alexie's work, this poem highlights the cross-cultural influences that can strengthen Native peoples.

Like Ali, Alexie tells it like it is. He idealizes neither Native nor American societies; rather, he stands for the truth. Native poets who have influenced him include Leslie Marmon Silko, Adrian C. Louis, Simon Ortiz, and Luci Tapahonso. Additional literary influences are named in his "Totem Sonnets," from *The Summer of Black Widows* (1996). They include Emily Dickinson, Flannery O'Connor, John Steinbeck, Walt Whitman, Zora Neale Hurston, Pablo Neruda, Edgar Bearchild (the fictional name of Ray Young Bear), and Jim Loney (a fictional character in a James Welch novel).

Alexie has no doubt been influenced by Allen Ginsberg, too. In Alexie's

"Defending Walt Whitman," which resembles Ginsberg's "Supermarket in California," Whitman in his "ludicrous" long beard plays basketball with Indian boys on the reservation. In this long-lined poem, Alexie imagines Whitman exclaiming, "Every body is brown! Look there, that boy can run / up and down the court forever. He can leap for a rebound / with his back arched like a salmon . . . / . . . / as if the court were a river, / as if the rim were a dam, as if the air were a ladder / leading the Indian boy toward home" (14). Like the salmon, the sacred food of the Spokane, the boys are beautiful, but both must climb ladders placed in their path by an alien culture. Yet Whitman, having come out of the nineteenth century, knows less about basketball than do the Indian boys. Maybe that is why Alexie can "defend" him, in both senses of the word. The final stanza begins, "God, there is beauty in every body," echoing Whitman's strongest theme. So, though "Whitman cannot tell the difference between / offense and defense" (15), at least he loves all the players. The poem ends, giving Whitman his due: "This game belongs to him" (15).

In "Things (for an Indian) to Do in New York (City)," the influences of Whitman and Ginsberg are obvious, but Alexie's consciousness is superimposed on theirs: " I stop bearded men / and beautiful women in the streets / and they're all poets. Everybody / is bearded and beautiful. Everybody is a poet" (125). Fully aware of America's literary tradition, Alexie writes of a drunk quoting Robert Frost and exclaims, "My God, he's home- / less and formalist" (125). Echoing Ginsberg, Alexie writes, "But, America, I think how / your men will always find / a more effective way to kill" (128). By the end of the poem, Alexie's attention is focused not on New York or America but on his Native identity: "There's an Indian / on the F Train all the way from Brooklyn / to Manhattan. She's my wife, and she loves me, / she loves me, she loves me" (130).

Back on the reservation, dams have been built, and only the ghosts of salmon remain in the dammed-out Spokane Falls, "That Place Where Ghosts of Salmon Jump." Alexie begins this poem with the Spokane myth of lovelorn Coyote, who was jealous of the salmon and smashed "a paw across the water of the Spokane River" to cause a rain that lasted forty days and forty nights and eventually Spokane Falls. Now that the falls have been dammed, they "sit dry / and quiet as a graveyard" (19).

Another devastating transformation of the Spokane environment, uranium mining has left the reservation people and animals poisoned with cancer. Alexie's "Haibun" addresses this nuclear-age history. Prose descriptions of uranium mining are interspersed with haiku images of traditional and modern Spokane culture. Uranium was discovered on the Spokane Reservation in 1954. For almost twenty years mining companies operated there, "dropping dust on the heads of Indian children standing beside the road. I remember waving to the truck drivers, who were all white men. I remember they always waved back. . . . I cannot tell you how many coffins we filled during the time of the trucks, but we learned to say 'cancer' like we said 'oxygen' and 'love'" (29). This description of radiation's terrible toll on human life is followed by the haiku "Grandmother died on her couch / covered with seven quilts, / one for each of her children" (29). Alexie has joined the older generation of poets—Ortiz, Hogan, and Silko—in exposing the human cost of the environmental exploitation of Indian land.

Alexie has responded enthusiastically to the work of other poets, such as Tiffany Midge, whose book *Outlaws, Renegades and Saints: Diary of a Mixed-Up Halfbreed* (1996) won the Diane Decorah Award in 1994. Established in 1992 in conjunction with the Returning the Gift Festival, a gathering of Native writers in Oklahoma that was organized by Joseph Bruchac, the award has been presented each year for a first book by a Native writer. Alexie's statement "Listen to this woman, she's got stories we all need to hear" appears on the back cover of Midge's book.

Born in 1965, Midge is an enrolled member of the Standing Rock Sioux Reservation, but she grew up in the Northwest. Her mother is Hunkpapa; her father is of German ancestry. Midge's poetry is the story of her own life and that of her extended family on the reservation and in the city of Seattle. It also provides political and social commentary on the larger American scene and is filled with the same kind of irony, humor, and references to pop culture found in the work of Alexie. Definitely contemporary, Midge's poetry comments insightfully on the broad impact of America's highly destructive culture. Her book is in four parts: "Pieces of Glass Resembling a Human Heart," "Nuclear Fission and the American Dream," "Trail of the

Outlaw's Tears," and "The Reflection of Reluctant Saints."

"Spare Change," a series of poems that open the book, focuses on Grandpa Dick, an elderly man who came to live with Midge's family when she was a girl. This man, who "lost his leg from a too-drunk stumbling / tumbling / mumbling fall on the gravel road leading to the neighborhood tavern" (8), nevertheless, through his insight and his sense of humor, "left us something to believe in. *Ourselves*" (4). And he even left the family money to live on in a desperate time. They had not believed him when he "claimed to be rich," but after he died, they "received a check for fifty-thousand dollars" from his oil-leased land in Montana (4). Grandpa Dick's ironic commentaries on white culture, she says, "changed us" (11). The first poem's epigraph, "—*Brother, can you spare a dime?,*" a familiar lyric from the Depression era, connects the Indian experience with the history and conditions of poverty in the United States.

"Diary of a Mixed-Up Halfbreed," which begins the second part of Midge's book, chronicles her childhood in a series of prose poems that cover almost twelve years of her life. Her parents' fighting becomes a metaphor for the cultural clashes between Natives and Euro-Americans. From "January, 1966":

> My father pulled our family tree up by the roots and separated us into two separate halves. He and I staked a claim in the Pacific Northwest, colonized unfamiliar territory like any ambitious pioneer would. Using me for ransom he coerced my mother into signing a treaty that would cut clean her traditional ties to the Dakota lands she knew and loved. (31)

Midge's poetry expresses so well not just the plight of the halfbreed but that of any child whose parents are "fighting like cowboys and Indians." "February, 1967" chronicles her feelings when only two years old:

> I don't know which side to take, either way I'm branded a traitor or renegade. I have no loyalty for either side. All I can do is sit divided somewhere in the middle of their war and wait for this damn rain to stop. Wait for the thunder to break and the clouds to separate into two equal parts that don't add up to the confusion in

my fractioned heart. (32)

Midge's commentary is more than personal; her political perspective is acute. In "September, 1974": "My parents split like atoms in a nuclear, free testing zone, finally exploded then walked around for the next few years trying to recover the lost parts of themselves" (40). A series of prose poems that make up her "Travel Diary" view the bizarre carnival atmosphere surrounding the Black Hills, the sacred center of the Lakota Nation, now promoted as a tourist destination:

> We drive to the "shrine." . . . Winnebago and Apache land cruisers are positioned randomly throughout the parking area, as if to say, *one man's shrine is another man's cemetery.* A bright ribbon of red paint is smeared across Washington's classic nose, as if to say, *goddamn, this elevation has given me a nosebleed.* Trapped within another mountain, several miles away, a warrior's arm is pointed towards the men's room, as if to say, *America is going to the toilet.* On our way out of Keystone, we stop at a souvenir shop. I can't resist buying the Indian bow, arrow and knife set, wrapped up in a slick package of artificial African leopard skin. (54)

In the third part of her book, Midge sees herself as the outlaw's daughter. Here she exploits the Western genre in poetic form, including a portrait, "Rodeo Queen," that may be a parody, but its language rings quite true:

> Forget your rules and tradition,
> your social teas, religion and pearl
> colored linens, I ain't like all the rest
> of your sisters, 'cuz I'm a rodeo queen,
> a cowgirl, a bulldogger. Whatever propriety I lack
> is your problem, 'cuz I always knew that I'd go far! (75)

The final poem in Midge's book, "Night of the Living Dead," is dedicated to Sherman Alexie. Midge views this well-known horror film as a metaphor for life in American culture:

I've failed to escape the certain horror of this picture
The inconsolable image the b-movie inflicted.
Some twenty years later I found myself asking—

what if?

What if the ghost dancers at Wounded Knee
were to rise from their mass grave
and turn the world upside-down?
Suppose delirious prophesies came true. (101)

The poem ends powerfully, *"listen, / can you hear the dead talking? /* They are saving and resurrecting us all" (104).

Like Midge and many other Native poets, Mahealani Dudoit recognizes the importance to survival of acknowledging the spirits. The editor of *'oiwi: a native hawaiian journal,* which she started in 1998, Dudoit begins and ends her essay "Carving a Hawaiian Aesthetic" with a prayer to the "ancestral gods." Affirming their connection to the ancient culture, contemporary poets such as Haunani-Kay Trask and Ku'ualoaha Meyer Ho'omanawanui, whose work is included in the first issue of *'oiwi,* acknowledge the ancestors, celebrating the natural beauty of the islands and decrying their destruction and pollution from colonization.

Trask's *Light in the Crevice Never Seen* (1994) was the first full-length book of poems by a Native Hawaiian to be published in North America. Trask graduated from the University of Wisconsin-Madison in 1981 with a Ph.D. in political science. A Hawaiian nationalist, she is professor of Hawaiian studies at the University of Hawaii in Manoa. Placing herself within the long continuum of the literature and life of the islands, Trask says in her preface, "My people have lived in the Hawaiian Islands since the time of Papa—Earth Mother—and Wakea—Sky Father." Pele, the volcanic goddess whose eruptions created the islands, is the metaphoric core of Trask's three-part book. Her "Chant of Lamentation," the title poem of the first part, laments the colonizers' destruction of her people and environment.

Like Ginsberg's *Kaddish*, Trask's book pays mournful respect to the victims of the desecrators, lamenting "wounded skies" of nuclear testing and war, "the black / and naked past, a million ghosts / laid out across the ocean floor," "the flowers / *a'ole pua*, without / issue on the stained / and dying earth" and her "own / long, furious lamentation" (24).

In the second part of her book, "Raw, Swift and Deadly," Trask condemns such atrocities as "those 5 gallon / toilets flushing / away tourist waste / into our waters" in her poem "Waikiki" (60). Other poems in this part describe the colonizers' attempts to acculturate the indigenous people and the often strained relations between Native Hawaiians and haole (white people) or other foreigners, such as the Japanese, who now live on the islands.

The poems in the third part, "Light in the Crevice Never Seen," rise above the lament and conflicted relations to celebrate the beauty of the natural elements, native plants, animals, and human beings that remain. "When the Rain Comes," spoken directly to the reader, leads you out "into the marsh," into full contact with the winds and the "great gray / clouds." By letting "the mist / wet your breasts" and flinging "off your / last piece of colored cloth," you again fall into the embrace of the island and are washed clean (85).

Recognizing in the 1970s that the voice of American Indian poets did not stop on the western edge of the turtle's back but continued onward to the Hawaiian Islands, editors Duane Niatum and Geary Hobson published poems by Dana Naone, a resident of Maui. Twenty years later, in "Looking for Signs," from Harjo and Bird's anthology *Reinventing the Enemy's Language*, Dana Naone Hall expresses her people's regard for a dusty road that is important in their mythology, memories, spirits, and physical life. The indigenous people's determination to keep the road open conflicts with the tourist industry: "The foreign owners of a half-built hotel don't want their guests / to taste the dust / of our ancestors in the road" (334). The road is on "the island where Maui / caught the sun in his rope" in the city of Makena. This is the *"old trail"* along which the people have always traveled to the ocean and mountain and to visit with one another. Hall describes the people like Aunty Alice, Tutu, Uncle Charley, and Ed, who live on the island, have always depended on the road, and are inseparable from the nature of the place that is essential to their Hawaiian consciousness. Of

Tutu, Hall writes, "She is old and small now / in her bed above the blue ocean / wrapped in the veil of her dream" (334). Natives of North America can perfectly understand the context and meaning of Hall's poem. The history of destruction, colonization, and exploitation has been repeated again and again as the colonists have staked their claims. Nevertheless, the indigenous people continue the "dream wheels" of their cultures on their voices and in their poetry.

From East-coast Mohawk poet and publisher Maurice Kenny to indigenous Hawaiians such as Haunani-Kay Trask, Native poets are sounding a powerful voice, one that will be heard long into the new millennium. Their poetry is accompanied by a rapidly expanding body of literary criticism. In the twenty-first century, as indigenous poetry from all over the earth is published, readers will notice many parallels between the poetry of Native Americans and that of other indigenous authors. These poets, who have inherited an ancient understanding of the lands and histories of human habitation, offer us a keen perspective on life in the modern, overly consumptive era. Their transformations of contemporary experience into poetry can help us find more creative and purposeful ways to live on this earth.

Bibliography

Alexie, Sherman. *The Business of Fancydancing: Stories and Poems.* Brooklyn: Hanging Loose Press, 1992.

———. *First Indian on the Moon.* Brooklyn: Hanging Loose Press, 1993.

———. *Old Shirts & New Skins.* Los Angeles: American Indian Studies Center, University of California, 1993.

———. *One Stick Song.* Brooklyn: Hanging Loose Press, 2000.

———. *Smoke Signals.* New York: Hyperion, 1998.

———. *The Summer of Black Widows.* Brooklyn: Hanging Loose Press, 1996.

Allan, Lewis. "Strange Fruit." In *The Ultimate Jazz Fakebook,* comp. by Herb Wong. Winona, Minn.: Hal Leonard, 1988, 364.

Allen, Paula Gunn. *The Sacred Hoop: Recovering the Feminine in American Indian Traditions.* Boston: Beacon Press, 1986.

———, ed. *Studies in American Indian Literature: Critical Essays and Course Designs.* New York: Modern Language Association of America, 1983.

Allen, Terry, ed. *The Whispering Wind: Poetry by Young American Indians.* Garden City, N.Y.: Doubleday, 1972.

Astrov, Margot, ed. *American Indian Prose and Poetry: An Anthology.* New York: Capricorn Books, 1962.

Attie, Jacob Freydont. "Interview with Lance Henson." *Cuyahoga: The Oberlin Quarterly* (Spring 1993): 24–29.

Barnes, Jim. *The American Book of the Dead: Poems.* Urbana: University of Illinois Press, 1982.

——. *La Plata Cantata: Poems.* West Lafayette, Ind.: Purdue University Press, 1989.

——. *The Sawdust War: Poems.* Urbana: University of Illinois Press, 1992.

——. *A Season of Loss: Poems.* West Lafayette, Ind.: Purdue University Press, 1985.

Bellm, Dan. "Ode to Joy." *Village Voice* (April 2, 1991): 78.

Bataille, Gretchen M., ed. *Native American Women: A Biographical Dictionary.* New York: Garland, 1993.

Bellinelli, Matteo, dir. *Native American Novelists, vol. 1, N. Scott Momaday.* Video recording. Princeton: Films for the Humanities and Sciences, 1995.

Berner, Robert L. "Lance Henson: Poet of the People." *World Literature Today* 64 (Summer 1990): 418–21.

Berthrong, Donald J. *The Cheyenne and Arapaho Ordeal: Reservation and Agency Life in the Indian Territory, 1875–1907.* Norman, Okla.: University of Oklahoma Press, 1976.

Bigjim, Fred. *Sinrock.* Portland, Ore.: Press-22, 1983.

Brill, Susan B. "Sherman Alexie." In *Dictionary of Literary Biography, 175, Native American Writers of the United States,* ed. Kenneth M. Roemer. Detroit: Gale Research, 1997, 3–10.

Bross, Jim. "He's product of Oxford, Yale, but Oklahoma is poet's forte." *The Norman* [Oklahoma] *Transcript,* October 21, 1976, 2.

Bruchac, Joseph. *Survival This Way: Interviews with American Indian Poets.* Tucson: Sun Tracks and University of Arizona Press, 1987.

——. "To Love the Earth: Some Thoughts on Walt Whitman." In *Walt Whitman: The Measure of His Song,* ed. Jim Perlman et al. Minneapolis: Holy Cow! Press, 1981, 274–78.

——, ed. *Returning the Gift: Poetry and Prose from the First North America Native Writers' Festival.* Tucson: University of Arizona Press, 1994.

Bucke, Richard M. *Cosmic Consciousness.* New York: E. P. Dutton, 1923.

Burlin, Natalie Curtis, ed. *The Indians' Book: An Offering by the American Indians of Indian Lore.* New York: Harper and Brothers, 1907.

Cameron, T. D. "The Conceptions Southwest interview with Lance Henson." *Conceptions Southwest* (Spring 1993): 24–28.

Churchill, Ward. *Struggle for the Land: Indigenous Resistance to Genocide, Ecocide, and Expropriation in Contemporary North America.* Monroe, Maine: Common Courage Press, 1993.

Clark, C. B. "Joy Harjo (Creek) b. 1951." In *The Heath Anthology of American Literature,* ed. Paul Lauter et al. 2 vols. Lexington, Mass.: D. C. Heath and Co., 1994, vol. 2, 3116–17.

Coltelli, Laura. *Winged Words: American Indian Writers Speak.* Lincoln: University of Nebraska Press, 1990.

Cook-Lynn, Elizabeth. "Anti-Indianism: A Literary Critique." *IKCE WICASTA: The Common People Journal,* 1, 4 (Winter 1999). 15–25.

———. *I Remember the Fallen Trees: New and Selected Poems.* Cheney, Wash.: Eastern Washington University Press, 1998.

———. *Seek the House of Relatives.* Marvin, S.Dak.: Blue Cloud Quarterly Press, 1983.

Davis, William T., ed. *Bradford's History of Plymouth Plantation.* New York: Charles Scribner's Sons, 1908.

Debo, Angie. *A History of the Indians of the United States.* Norman, Okla.: University of Oklahoma Press, 1970.

Deloria, Vine, Jr. *Custer Died for Your Sins; An Indian Manifesto.* New York: Macmillan, 1969.

Densmore, Frances, ed. *Music of Acoma, Isleta, Cochiti and Zuñi Pueblos.* Smithsonian Institution Bureau of American Ethnology. Washington, D.C.: Government Printing Office, 1957; reprint ed., New York: Da Capo Press, 1972.

Dodge, Robert, and Joseph B. McCullough, eds. *Voices from Wah'Kon-Tah; Contemporary Poetry of Native Americans.* New York: International Publishers, 1974.

Dudoit, D. Mahealani. "Carving an Hawaiian Aesthetic." *'oiwi: a native hawaiian journal.* 1, 1 (December 1998): 20–26.

Durham, Jimmie. *Columbus Day: Poems, Drawings and Stories about American Indian Life and Death in the Nineteen-seventies.* Minneapolis: West End Press, 1983.

Evers, Larry, and Ofelia Zepeda, eds. *Home Places: Contemporary Native American Writing from* Sun Tracks. Tucson: University of Arizona Press, 1995.

Faderman, Lillian, and Barbara Bradshaw, comps. *Speaking for Ourselves: American Ethnic Writing.* Glenview, Ill.: Scott, Foresman, 1975.

Fire, John/Lame Deer and Richard Erdoes. *Lame Deer: Seeker of Visions.* New York: Pocket Books, 1976.

Fletcher, Alice C., and Francis La Flesche. *The Omaha Tribe.* 27th Annual Report of the Bureau of American Ethnology, 1905–6. Washington, D.C.: Government Printing Office, 1911.

Gibson, Arrell M. *The Chickasaws.* Norman, Okla.: University of Oklahoma Press, 1971.

Gogisgi/Carroll Arnett. "Lance (David) Henson." In *Dictionary of Native American Literature,* ed. Andrew Wiget. New York: Garland, 1994, 441–43.

Harjo, Joy. "Bio-poetics Sketch for Greenfield Review." *Greenfield Review,* 9, 3–4 (Winter 1981/82): 8–9.

———. "Fire." In *The Woman That I Am: The Literature and Culture of Contemporary Women of Color,* ed. D. Soyini Madison. New York: St. Martin's Press, 1994, 3.

——. *Fishing*. Browerville, Minn.: Ox Head Press, 1992.

——. "Four Poems." *American Poetry Review*, 28, 3 (May/June 1999): 31–32.

——. *The Last Song*. Las Cruces, N.M.: Puerto del Sol Press, 1975.

——. *In Mad Love and War*. Middletown, Conn.: Wesleyan University Press, 1990.

——. *A Map to the Next World: Poetry and Tales*. New York: W. W. Norton & Co., 2000.

——. "Ordinary Spirit." In *I Tell You Now: Autobiographical Essays by Native American Writers*, ed. Brian Swann and Arnold Krupat (Lincoln: University of Nebraska Press, 1987), 263–70.

——. *Secrets from the Center of the World*. Sun Tracks Series, vol. 17. Tucson: University of Arizona Press, 1989.

——. *She Had Some Horses*. New York: Thunder's Mouth Press, 1983.

——. "Three Generations of Native American Women's Birth Experience." *Ms.* 2, 1 (July–August 1991): 28–30.

——. *What Moon Drove Me to This?* New York: I. Reed Books, 1979.

——. "The Woman Hanging from the Thirteenth Floor Window." *Wicazo Sa Review*, 1, 1 (Spring 1985): 38–40.

——. *The Woman Who Fell from the Sky: Poems*. New York: W. W. Norton, 1996.

——. "Writing with the Sun." In *Where We Stand: Women Poets on Literary Tradition*, ed. Sharon Bryan. New York: W. W. Norton, 1993, 70–74.

—— and Gloria Bird, eds. *Reinventing the Enemy's Language: Contemporary Native Women's Writings of North America*. New York: W. W. Norton, 1997.

—— and Poetic Justice. *Letter from the End of the Twentieth Century*. Albuquerque: Red Horse Records, 1996.

Henson, Lance. *Un Altro Canzione per L'America* (translation). Milan: Edizione Del'Arco, 1992.

——. *Another Distance: New and Selected Poems*. Norman, Okla.: Point Riders Press, 1991.

——. *Another Song for America*. Norman, Okla.: Cottonwood Arts Foundation, Point Riders Press, dist., 1987.

——. *Buffalo Marrow on Black*. Edmond, Okla.: Full Count Press, 1979.

——. *A Cheyenne Sketchbook: Selected Poems 1970–1991*. Greenfield Center, N.Y.: Greenfield Review Press, 1985, 1992.

——. *A Circling Remembrance: Poems*. Marvin, S.Dak.: Blue Cloud Quarterly Press, 1984.

——. *In a Dark Mist*. Merrick, N.Y.: Cross Cultural Communications, 1992.

——. "Journal Entries." *Poetry East* 32 (Fall 1991): 51–52.

——. *Keeper of Arrows*. Johnstown, Pa.: Renaissance Press, 1971; rev. ed., Renaissance with Walking Badger Press, 1972.

——. *Le Orme del Tasso/The Badger Tracks*. Turin: Soconos Incomindios, 1989.

——. *Mistah: New Poems*. New York: Strawberry Press, 1977.

——. *A Motion of Sudden Aloneness: Expatriot Songs*. Little Rock: American Native Press Archives/University of Arkansas at Little Rock, 1991.

——. *Naming the Dark: Poems for the Cheyenne*. Norman, Okla.: Point Riders Press, 1976.

——. *Poems for a Master Beadworker*. Osnabruck, Germany: OBMA, 1993.

——. *Revolutionslied*. Milan: Selene Edizioni, 1998.

——. *Selected Poems, 1970–83*. Greenfield Center, N.Y.: Greenfield Review Press, 1985.

——. *Strong Heart Song: Lines from a Revolutionary Text: Poetry*. Albuquerque: West End Press, 1997.

——. *Teepee*. Chivasso, Italy: Cooperative La Parentesi/Soconos Incomindios, 1987.

——. *This Small Sound/Dieser Kleine Klang*. German trans. by Hartmut Lutz. Berlin: Institut für Indianische Kulturen Nordamericas, 1987.

——. *Tonger Ut Stiennen/Thunder From Stones*. Friesian trans. by Jelle Kaspersma. Leeuwarden, Netherlands: Fryske Nasjonale Partij, 1987.

——. *Trail Buio e la Luce/Between the Dark and the Light*. Milan: Selene Edizioni, 1993.

—— and Lisa Schnorf. *Lieder in der Sprache des Feindes/Songs in the Enemy's Language*. Munich: Big Mountain Aktionsgruppe, 1999.

Hobson, Geary. *The Remembered Earth: An Anthology of Contemporary Native American Literature*. Albuquerque: University of New Mexico Press, 1981.

Hogan, Linda. Autobiographical statement in *Sun Tracks*, 5 (1979): 78.

——. *The Book of Medicines: Poems*. Minneapolis: Coffee House Press, 1993.

——. *Calling Myself Home*. Greenfield Center, N.Y.: Greenfield Review Press, 1978.

——. *Daughters, I Love You*. Denver: Research Center on Women, 1981.

——. *Eclipse*. Los Angeles: American Indian Studies Center, University of California, 1983.

——. "The 19th Century Native American Poets." *Wassaja* 13, 4 (November 1980): 24–29.

——. *Red Clay: Poems and Stories*. Greenfield Center, N.Y.: Greenfield Review Press, 1991.

——. *Savings: Poems*. Minneapolis: Coffee House Press, 1988.

——. *Seeing Through the Sun*. Amherst: University of Massachusetts Press, 1985.

——. "To Light." In *Harper's Anthology of 20th Century Native American Poetry*, ed. Duane Niatum. San Francisco: Harper & Row, 1988.

——. "Who Puts Together." In *Studies in American Indian Literature*, ed. Paula Gunn Allen. New York: Modern Language Association of America, 1983.

Jackson, Helen Hunt. *A Century of Dishonor*. New York: Harper and Brothers, 1881.

Jaimes, M. Annette, ed. *The State of Native America: Genocide, Colonization and Resistance*. Boston: South End Press, 1992.

Johansen, Bruce. *Native American Political Systems and the Evolution of Democracy: An Annotated Bibliography.* Westport, Conn.: Greenwood Press, 1996.

Kallet, Marilyn. "In Love and War." *Kenyon Review* 15, 3 (Summer 1993): 57–66.

Kaye, Howard. "The Post-Symbolist Poetry of Yvor Winters." *The Southern Review* New Series 1 (January 1971): 180–81.

Kenny, Maurice. *Blackrobe; Isaac Jogues, b. March 11, 1604, d. October 18, 1646: Poems.* Saranac Lake, N.Y.: North Country Community College Press, 1982.

———. *Dancing Back Strong the Nation: Poems.* Marvin, S.Dak.: Blue Cloud Quarterly Press, 1979; rev. ed., Buffalo: White Pine, 1979.

———. *Greyhounding This America: Poems and Dialog.* Chico, Calif.: Heidelberg Graphics, 1988.

———. *The Mama Poems.* Buffalo: White Pine, 1984.

———. *North: Poems of Home.* Marvin, S.Dak.: Blue Cloud Quarterly, 1977.

———. *On Second Thought: A Compilation.* Norman, Okla.: Univ. of Oklahoma Press, 1995.

La Flesche, Francis. *The Osage Tribe Rite of the Chiefs; Sayings of the Ancient Men.* Smithsonian Institution 36th Annual Report of the Bureau of American Ethnology. Washington, D.C.: Government Printing Office, 1914–15.

Lawrence, D. H. *Studies in Classic American Literature.* New York: Viking Press, 1964.

Long Wolf, Tony, Jr. "THE ELECTRICAL HISTORIAN THAT WILL REPLACE THE OLD FOLKS AND THEIR STORIES BY THE CAMP FIRE AND WE CAN STILL HAVE BUFFALO SOUP AND CRACKERS—AFTERWARDS!!!!" *Vermillion Literary Project* 8 (1990): 20–21.

Louis, Adrian C. *Among the Dog Eaters: Poems.* Albuquerque: West End Press, 1992.

———. *Fire Water World: Poems.* Albuquerque: West End Press, 1989.

McDermott, Maura. "A Harvest of Native Poets." *Oklahoma Today* 43: 5 (September–October 1993): 42–47.

Maddocks, Melvin. *Billie Holiday: Biography and Notes on the Music.* Alexandria, Va.: Time-Life Records, 1979.

Matthiessen, Peter. *In the Spirit of Crazy Horse.* New York: Viking Press, 1983.

Midge, Tiffany. *Outlaws, Renegades and Saints: Diary of a Mixed-Up Halfbreed.* Greenfield Center, N.Y.: Greenfield Review Press, 1996.

Milton, John R., ed. *The American Indian Speaks.* Vermillion, S.Dak.: Dakota Press, 1969.

Momaday, N. Scott. *Angle of Geese and Other Poems.* Boston: David R. Godine, 1974.

———. *The Complete Poems of Frederick Goddard Tuckerman.* New York: Oxford University Press, 1965.

———. "A First American Views His Land." *National Geographic* 150, 1 (1976):

13–18.

———. *The Gourd Dancer*. New York: Harper & Row, 1976.

———. *In the Bear's House*. New York: St. Martin's Press, 1999.

———. *In the Presence of the Sun: Stories and Poems, 1961-1991*. New York: St. Martin's Press, 1992.

———. *The Man Made of Words: Essays, Stories, Passages*. New York: St. Martin's Press, 1997.

———. *The Names: A Memoir*. New York: Harper & Row, 1976.

———. *The Way to Rainy Mountain*. Albuquerque: University of New Mexico Press, 1969.

Moore, David L. "Ray A. Young Bear." *Dictionary of Literary Biography, 175, Native American Writers of the United States*, ed. Kenneth M. Roemer. Detroit: Gale Research, 1997, 322–30.

Mooney, James. *The Ghost-Dance Religion and the Sioux Outbreak of 1890*. 14th Annual Report of the Bureau of Ethnology. Washington, D.C.: Government Printing Office, 1896.

Niatum, Duane, ed. *Harper's Anthology of 20th Century Native American Poetry*. San Francisco: Harper & Row, 1988.

———. "Warrior Artists of the Southern Plains." *Michigan Quarterly Review* 29 (1990): 406–9.

Ortiz, Simon J. *After and Before the Lightning*. Tucson: University of Arizona Press, 1994.

———. *Fight Back: For the Sake of the People, For the Sake of the Land*. Albuquerque: Institute for Native American Development, Native American Studies, University of New Mexico, 1980.

———. *From Sand Creek*. New York: Thunder's Mouth Press, 1981; 2nd ed., Tucson: University of Arizona Press, 1999.

———. *Going for the Rain: Poems*. New York: Harper & Row, 1976.

———. Interview with Shirley Sneve. *The Circle: Hocoka*. Television program, South Dakota Public Television. KUSD, Vermillion, S.Dak., 1985.

———. "The Language We Know." In *I Tell You Now*, ed. Brian Swann and Arnold Krupat. Lincoln: University of Nebraska Press, 1987, 185–94.

———. *Woven Stone*. Tucson: University of Arizona Press, 1992.

Parman, Frank. Review of *In Mad Love and War*. *The Gayly Oklahoman* (December 1990): 11.

Revard, Carter. *Cowboys and Indians, Christmas Shopping*. Norman, Okla.: Point Riders Press, 1992.

———. "The Coyote." *The Massachusetts Review* 1, 4 (1960): 634.

———. *An Eagle Nation*. Tucson: University of Arizona Press, 1993.

———. *Family Matters, Tribal Affairs*. Tucson: University of Arizona Press, 1998.

———. *My Right Hand Don't Leave Me No More*. St. Louis: EEDIN Press, 1970.

——. *Nonymosity.* Richfield, Vt.: Samisdat, 1980.

——. *Ponca War Dancers.* Norman, Okla.: Point Riders Press, 1980.

——. "Traditional Osage Naming Ceremonies: Entering the Circle of Being." In *Recovering the Word: Essays on Native American Literature,* ed. Brian Swann and Arnold Krupat. Berkeley and Los Angeles: University of California Press, 1987, 446–66.

——. *Winning the Dust Bowl.* Tucson: University of Arizona Press, 2001.

Roemer, Kenneth M., ed. *Dictionary of Literary Biography, Vol. 175: Native American Writers of the United States.* Detroit: Gale Research, 1997.

Rose, Wendy. *Academic Squaw.* Marvin, S.Dak.: Blue Cloud Quarterly, 1977.

——. *Bone Dance: New and Selected Poems, 1965-1993.* Tucson: University of Arizona Press, 1994.

——. *Builder Kachina: A Home-Going Cycle.* Marvin, S.Dak.: Blue Cloud Quarterly, 1979.

——. *The Halfbreed Chronicles and Other Poems.* Los Angeles: West End Press, 1985.

——. *Hopi Roadrunner Dancing.* Greenfield Center, N.Y.: Greenfield Review Press, 1973.

——. *Long Division: A Tribal History.* New York: Strawberry Press, 1976; rev. ed., 1981.

——. *Lost Copper: Poems.* Banning, Calif.: Malki Museum Press, 1980.

——. *Now Poof She Is Gone: Poetry.* Ithaca, N.Y.: Firebrand Books, 1994.

——. *What Happened When the Hopi Hit New York.* New York: Contact II Publications, 1982.

Rosen, Kenneth M., ed. *The Man to Send Rain Clouds: Contemporary Stories by American Indians.* New York: Viking Press, 1974.

Ruoff, A. LaVonne Brown. *American Indian Literatures: An Introduction, Bibliographic Review, and Selected Bibliography.* New York: Modern Language Association of America, 1990.

——. Introduction to E. Pauline Johnson, *The Moccasin Maker.* Tucson: University of Arizona Press, 1987, 1–37.

Rushforth, Scott, and Steadman Upham. *A Hopi Social History: Anthropological Perspectives on Sociocultural Persistence and Change.* Austin: University of Texas Press, 1992.

Sale, Kirkpatrick. *The Conquest of Paradise: Christopher Columbus and the Columbian Legacy.* New York: Alfred A. Knopf, 1990.

Savageau, Cheryl. *Dirt Road Home: Poems.* Willimantic, Conn.: Curbstone Press, 1995.

Scarry, John. "Representing Real Worlds: The Evolving Poetry of Joy Harjo." *World Literature Today* 66, 2 (Spring 1992): 286–91.

Schwab, Tim, and Christine Craton. *Ghost Dance: A Film by Tim Schwab and Christine Craton.* Videocassette. New York: New Day Films, 1991.

Smelcer, John E., and D. L. Birchfield, eds. *Durable Breath: Contemporary Native American Poetry.* Anchorage: Salmon Run Press, 1994.

Smith, Patricia Clark, with Paula Gunn Allen. "Earthly Relations, Carnal Knowledge: Southwestern American Indian Women Writers and Landscape." In *The Desert Is No Lady,* ed. Vera Norwood and Janice Monk (New Haven, Conn.: Yale University Press, 1987, 174–96.

Smith, Stephanie Izarek. "Joy Harjo." *Poets and Writers Magazine* 21, 4 (July-August 1993): 22–27.

Spinden, Herbert Joseph, ed. and trans. *Songs of the Tewa.* New York: Exposition of Indian Tribal Arts, 1933.

Swann, Brian, and Arnold Krupat, eds. *I Tell You Now: Autobiographical Essays by Native American Writers.* Lincoln: University of Nebraska Press, 1987.

Terrell, John Upton. *Pueblos, Gods and Spaniards.* New York: Dial Press, 1973.

Trask, Haunani-Kay. *Light in the Crevice Never Seen.* Corvallis, Ore.: Calyx Books, 1994.

Trout, Lawana, comp. *Native American Literature: An Anthology.* Lincolnwood, Ill.: NTC Pub. Group, 1999.

Turner, Frederick W. *Beyond Geography: The Western Spirit Against the Wilderness.* New York: Viking Press, 1980.

———. Introduction to *I Have Spoken: American History through the Voices of the Indians,* ed. Virginia Armstrong. Chicago: Swallow Press, 1971, ix–xviii.

———. *Spirit of Place: The Making of an American Literary Landscape.* San Francisco: Sierra Club Books, 1989.

Weaver, Roger. Review of Lance Henson, *Another Song for America. Studies in American Indian Literatures* 4: 4 (Winter 1992): 102–4.

Whiteman, Roberta Hill. "Conversation Overheard on Tamalpais Road." In *The Third Woman,* ed. Dexter Fisher. Boston: Houghton Mifflin, 1980, 124–25.

———. *Philadelphia Flowers: Poems.* Duluth, Minn.: Holy Cow! Press, 1996.

———. *Star Quilt: Poems.* Minneapolis: Holy Cow! Press, 1984.

Wiget, Andrew. *Native American Literature.* Boston: Twayne Publishers, 1985.

———, ed. *Dictionary of Native American Literature.* New York: Garland, 1994.

———, trans. "The Singer's Art." In *Heath Anthology of American Literature,* ed. Paul Lauter et al. Lexington, Mass.: D. C. Heath & Co., 1994, 93–94.

Wilson, Norma C. "Beyond False Boundaries." *Studies in American Indian Literatures* 6, 1 (Spring 1994):71–82.

———. "Elizabeth Cook-Lynn," "Joy Harjo," and "Lance Henson." *Dictionary of Literary Biography, 175, Native American Writers of the United States,* ed. Kenneth M. Roemer. Detroit: Gale Research, 1997, 38–42, 112–18, 119–22.

———. "Heartbeat: Within the Visionary Tradition." In *Walt Whitman of Mickle Street,* ed. Geoffrey Sill. Knoxville: University of Tennessee Press, 1994, 224–35.

——. "Joy Harjo Brings Poetic Justice to South Dakota." *People's Culture* New Series 38 (1997): 3.

——. "Joy Harjo," "Linda Henderson Hogan," "Wendy Rose," and "Roberta Hill Whiteman." In *Handbook of Native American Literature,* ed. Andrew Wiget. New York: Garland, 1996, 437–44, 449–52, 495–98, and 539–43.

——. "Nesting in the Ruins." In *English Postcoloniality: Literatures from Around the World,* ed. R. Mohnanram and G. Rajan. Westport, Conn.: Greenwood Press, 1996, 179–87.

——. "Turtles and Learning to Be a Human: an Interview with Linda Hogan." *English Notes* 25, 3 (May 1980): 6–11.

Winters, Yvor. *Forms of Discovery; Critical & Historical Essays on the Forms of the Short Poem in English.* Chicago: Alan Swallow, 1967.

——. *The Function of Criticism: Problems and Exercises.* Denver: Alan Swallow, 1957.

Witt, Shirley Hill, and Stan Steiner, eds. *The Way: An Anthology of American Indian Literature.* New York: Vintage Books, 1972.

Womack, Craig. Review of Lance Henson, *Another Distance. American Indian Quarterly* 7: 1 (Winter 1993): 108.

Woody, Elizabeth. *Hand into Stone.* New York: Contact II, 1990.

——. *Luminaries of the Humble.* Tucson: University of Arizona Press, 1994.

——. *Seven Hands, Seven Hearts: Prose and Poetry.* Portland, Ore.: Eighth Mountain Press, 1994.

Young Bear, Ray A. *The Invisible Musician: Poems.* Duluth, Minn.: Holy Cow! Press, 1990.

——. *Winter of the salamander: the keeper of importance.* San Francisco: Harper & Row, 1980.

Zimmerman, Larry J. *Native North America.* Boston: Little, Brown, 1996.

Index

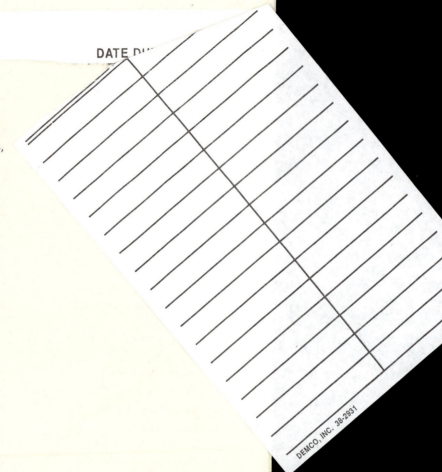

DATE DUE

DEMCO, INC. 38-2931